"THE BEST THINGS THAT COME OUT OF THE GARDEN ARE GIFTS FOR OTHER PEOPLE."

— JAMIE JOBB

To Renee,
Eat well!

BELLEVUE
*Farmers*
MARKET
COOKBOOK

*Cindy Pigott*

CINDY PIGOTT

FOREWORD BY CHEF HOLLY SMITH

DOCUMENTARY MEDIA
SEATTLE, WASHINGTON

Bellevue Farmers Market Cookbook

Published by Documentary Media LLC
3250 41st Ave SW
Seattle, WA 98116
(206) 935-9292
books@docbooks.com
www.documentarymedia.com

First edition, 2009

Printed in China

Author: Cindy Pigott
Foreword: Holly Smith
Photography: Cindy Pigott
Editor: Judy Gouldthorpe
Book Design and Illustration: Jon Cannell Design
Executive Editor: Barry Provorse
Publisher: Petyr Beck

Library of Congress Cataloging-in-Publication Data

Pigott, Cindy.
Bellevue Farmers Market cookbook / Cindy Pigott ; foreword by Holly Smith. -- 1st ed.
p. cm.
Includes bibliographical references and index.
ISBN 978-1-933245-16-4 (alk. paper)
1. Cookery, American. 2. Cookery--Washington (State)--Seattle.  I. Title.
TX715.P625 2009
641.59797'772--dc22
2009005185

TO MY DAUGHTERS
KERRY AND TURNER
WHO BRING ME SUNSHINE
EVEN IN THE RAIN

**FOREWORD**

P. 8

**MARKET HISTORY**

P. 10

**MARKET TIPS**

P. 12

**MARKET STAPLES**

P. 96

**MARKET VENDORS**

P. 123

**BIBLIOGRAPHY**

P. 126

MAY / JUNE

P. 14

JULY / AUGUST

P. 42

SEPTEMBER / OCTOBER

P. 72

ACKNOWLEDGMENTS

P. 129

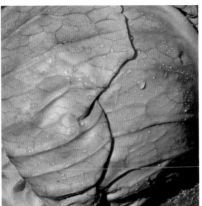

INDEX

P. 130

TABLE OF EQUIVALENTS

P. 134

## FOREWORD

By Chef Holly Smith, Café Juanita

I'm hooked! I am a farmers' market junkie and proud of it. What a joy it is to live in a community that appreciates and seeks out the best local food. I believe that the Seattle area is leading the way in taking back control of our food and in respecting ourselves, our farmers, and our land, unlike many other cities in the United States today. Not only do I want to be a part of this movement, but I also want to shout to the world, "Hey look — it tastes good and it's doable."

My favorite day off is usually one spent traipsing up and down the path at any of our great Seattle metropolitan markets — praying for sunshine and maybe a glimpse of Veraci's pizza oven! I found myself dreaming up ways to join in the fun not long ago, and happily, Poco Carretto Gelato was born with Bellevue Farmers Market in mind. I wanted to be part of the community — play in the outdoors and reap the benefits of all our local bounty. At Café Juanita, I am not able to be quite so in the moment and flexible as the market environment allows. That said, this touchstone to the local markets has impacted our food at Café Juanita as well. Market shopping is the gift that keeps on giving.

The recipes within this book represent this community. How fortunate we are to be able to find on any given market day the best tomatoes from small farms in eastern Washington, amazing local cheeses, meats, and seafood. The excitement is palpable, and the dedication to providing a vibrant marketplace is at its best at the Bellevue Farmers Market.

I encourage you to play with the recipes within and to bring your own market experience to the process of cooking. Shop with an open mind and your cooking will benefit. Be ready to try something new; maybe sunchokes or salsify or fava beans have never made it home but should this season.

I look forward to seeing you at the market, and I applaud the passion and determination that leads you there weekly. We can take back our food culture and make it stronger and more sustainable — and my goodness, it is a tasty journey!

Cheers,

Holly

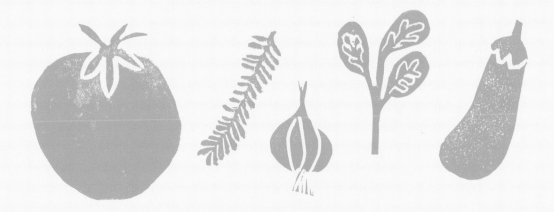

## MARKET HISTORY

For centuries, farmers' markets have been a part of the everyday life of villages, towns, and cities. The English colonists were the first to have a market in what would become the United States, way back in 1634. They and those who followed brought with them the familiarity of the markets back in their European homelands. The original proclamation for Philadelphia's market of 1693 states that the market shall be opened with the ringing of bells.

Fast-forward a few hundred years to June 17, 2004. That was the first day of Bellevue's very own farmers' market , and it too was opened by the ringing of a bell, joyfully, by Lori Taylor, the guiding force behind the market.

It was a year earlier that Lori, a Bellevue native who had spent many a summer visiting her grandparents on their dairy farm, was listening to Dr. Scott Dudley encourage his church congregation to explore ways to serve the Bellevue community and beyond. During this time of reflection, Lori came up with the idea of a farmers' market to take place right in the church parking lot. Oddly enough, around 1925, vineyards were the landscape of the very parking lot where the market would be held. Bellevue has quite an agricultural history, and up until the early 1940s, there were at least 80 farms between Lake Washington and Lake Sammamish.

For a year, Lori researched farmers' markets — from attending many of King County's markets to talking with the knowledgeable people at the Neighborhood Farmers Market Alliance. Lori was specific about what she wanted the Bellevue market to bring to the community. She wanted a market that focused on food and its growers. And like the Alliance, Lori wanted the market to support Washington's small family farms. It would be a venue to educate the community on the advantages of buying locally — both the health benefits of eating farm-fresh foods and the environmental benefits of helping to preserve these diminishing farmlands. Lori visited many of the farms, wanting to know what they were growing and how they were growing it, and even more important, learning about the growers themselves. She is close to many of the market's vendors. Given such dedication, it is no surprise that by the end of its inaugural year, the Bellevue Farmers Market had made it to the top three in the state for record sales in an opening season.

Recently, Lori found the sheet of paper where she had penned her thoughts about her vision of giving back to Bellevue. She had written that she wanted to bring joy to her community. It was an incredible feeling when years later, during a market Thursday, Lori overheard a shopper saying that the market was such a "joy" to come to each week.

Lori states: "To think that we are actually making a difference in people's lives is quite something. I continue to be amazed each week at what shows up on that asphalt parking lot. We are seeing the freshest and best of farm products in the state . . . it's a simple, incredible gift. There is a beauty to this way of life that I can't put my finger on or express in words. It's all wrapped up in the stewardship of the land, honest hard work, perseverance and dedication, the gift of food and how it brings people together. Something happens on market day, when urban and rural collide. A celebration takes place in the midst of diversity, and food is the common thread — food that sustains us, comforts us, and awakens our senses."

# "DON'T BE AFRAID TO GO OUT ON A LIMB . . . THAT'S WHERE THE FRUIT IS." — ANONYMOUS

# MARKET TIPS

1. If you know what you want and you know that it sells out fast, get to the market early. Remember, the market doesn't open until the bell rings! Bring a book to read while in line or enjoy the market's newsletter, available at the entrances.

2. If you aren't in a hurry, come later to the market and avoid the opening rush to the eggs!

3. Walk around the market once, just looking. Take in all the great colors, shapes, and smells. See what's new and fresh for that day.

4. Try to shop heavy to light, so delicate items don't get crushed.

5. Get to know the farmers. Don't be afraid to ask them about their products and how to cook them. You may end up with a new favorite recipe!

6. If you're offered a sample, give it a try. Even if you sat at the table for hours refusing to take a bite of something as a child, be adventuresome. Your taste buds may have changed, and you could be missing out on a wonderful, healthy treat.

7. Although some vendors accept credit cards, try to bring cash, preferably small bills.

8. Be patient. Sometimes everyone seems to be after the same thing at the same time. Take this moment in line to talk to the other shoppers about what they are buying and how they prepare it. Listen to the vendor's conversations with the ones ahead of you. You may learn something new or may be able to pass on some knowledge of your own.

9. If you aren't going home soon after shopping, try to remember to bring a cooler to keep your foods at their freshest. Also, if you are buying flowers, ask the farmers to put them in a bag with some water. They want you to enjoy their flowers as much as they enjoy growing them. Bring a bucket in your car to place them in to get them home in perfect shape.

10. Ask vendors if they offer farm tours. Washington State has a harvest celebration, usually in late September or early October, that many farmers participate in to showcase their farms. Experience their lives and what they do to bring you fresh foods. Let children learn where their food comes from — that it's not just from the grocery store aisle!

11. Enjoy your community at the market. It's a great place to meet a friend to go shopping or enjoy a bite to eat. You will probably see many people that you know, or you may make new friendships at the market. If you have the time, volunteer. It's a good way to get connected to the market and community and to get to know the farmers even better.

12. Finally, remember that you shop at a farmers' market for freshness, so eat what you buy as soon as possible for the freshest flavor.

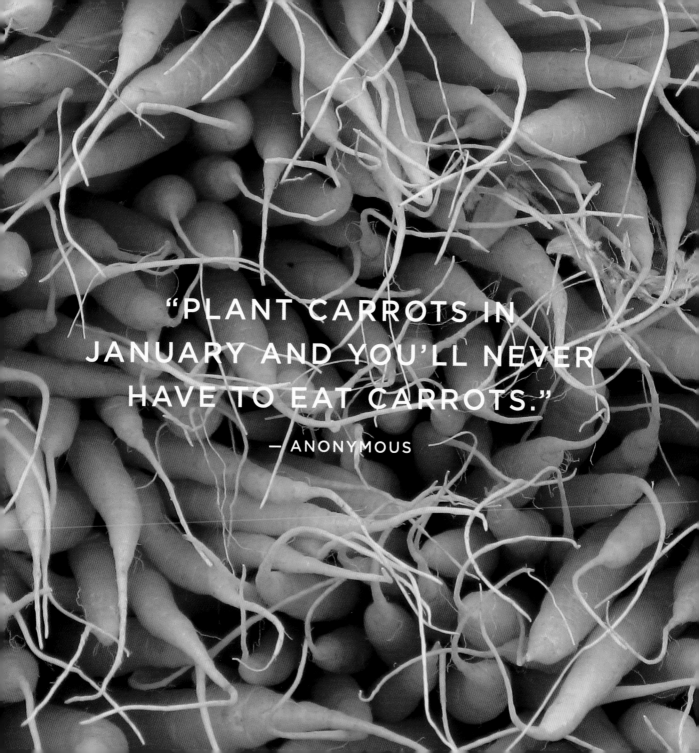

"PLANT CARROTS IN JANUARY AND YOU'LL NEVER HAVE TO EAT CARROTS."

—ANONYMOUS

MAY
JUNE

**EARLY-SEASON HARVEST**

**FROM THE SOURCE: PIPITONE FARMS**

**RECIPES:**

CARROT SOUP

ENGLISH PEA SOUP WITH MINTED RICOTTA AND MORELS

GRILLED ASPARAGUS WITH HAZELNUT AIGRELETTE AND PINOT NOIR SYRUP

BEET SOUFFLÉ

KAI'S TABBOULEH

AMERICAN WAGYU TENDERLOIN WITH SOY-MADEIRA GLAZED MUSHROOMS

STEAMED CLAMS WITH SWEET BASIL PESTO

PAN-SEARED SALMON AND BING CHERRIES

STRAWBERRY-RHUBARB CRUMBLE

APRICOT CHEESECAKE

### Apricots

Pick: Use your nose to choose the best apricots! They should have a delicate "apricot" smell and, when pressed between your fingers, should feel soft. Avoid light yellow fruit with a greenish tinge — they were picked too soon and will spoil before they reach their best flavor. Often, the deeper the color, the sweeter the apricot.

Pack: To keep them most flavorful, do not refrigerate, but do store in a cool place for up to five days. If they are very ripe and you want to keep them longer, store in the fridge for a couple of days. To ripen, put apricots in a loosely closed paper bag with an apple or banana. The other fruits give off a gas that quickens the ripening process.

Prep: Rinse unpeeled fruit in cold water. To split, slice around the seam, twist the halves in opposite directions, and pull apart. Remove the stone.

### Apriums

Pick: Apriums are 75 percent apricot/25 percent plum; they are usually yellow-skinned. Choose apriums that are plump and somewhat firm but give a little to slight pressure.

Pack: Store not-quite-ripe fruit in a loosely closed paper bag, away from sunlight. Once they've ripened, keep them loose in the crisper drawer of the fridge for up to a week.

Prep: Wash under cold running water. Most can be cut all the way through, or slice along the seam, twist the halves in opposite directions, and pull apart.

### Arugula

Pick: Familiarly known as "rocket" in the United Kingdom, this peppery green's younger leaves are the best. Older greens tend to be a bit tougher and spicier.

Pack: Rinse the leaves in cool water, wrap in a paper towel, and store in a plastic bag in the crisper drawer of the fridge. Use within four days.

Prep: Wash and trim the ends.

### Asparagus

Pick: The thinner the spear, usually the younger and more tender the asparagus. No matter what size you prefer, look for firm stems with tightly closed tops and whose cut ends are not dry.

Pack: With heads up, submerge the ends only in water and refrigerate, or wrap the ends in a moist paper towel in a plastic bag and store in the crisper drawer of the fridge for up to three days.

Prep: Rinse with cold water. Hold each spear with one hand toward the tip, the other near the base, and bend. The stem should break where the stalk starts to toughen.

## Bamboo Shoots (Takenoko)

Pick: Young, crisp shoots are the most tender.

Pack: Place whole, unpeeled shoots in the crisper drawer of the fridge for up to two weeks — any longer and they may become too bitter.

Prep: Do not eat raw — the shoots are too bitter and hard to digest. Trim the roots and peel away the outer leaves and any tough outer flesh. Boil whole or thinly sliced for at least five minutes to release a toxin. If they're still too bitter-tasting, boil again.

## Bavarian Horseradish

Pick: Choose a firm root without mold or soft spots.

Pack: Wrap a damp paper towel around the root. Place in a plastic bag and store in the crisper drawer of the fridge for up to 10 days.

Prep: Wash, then pare away the outer skin. Underneath the brown peel is a creamy white flesh that is usually grated into recipes.

## Beets and Beet Greens

Pick: The best beet has the freshest-looking greens. If the greens look healthy, it's a good indication that the roots will be moist and fresh as well. If the beets still have their greens attached, pick the bunch with the smallest leaves; if there are no greens, look for bulbs that appear moist, with no cracks, and aren't shriveled. The small to medium beets are usually more tender.

Pack: Store unwashed beets and beet greens separately in plastic bags in the crisper drawer of the fridge. Leave one to two inches of greens on the bulb to help keep the color from bleeding while cooking. The bulbs should keep for up to three weeks. The greens will last only a few days.

Prep: Wash the beets without removing the skin. This will help retain their color. Peeling the beets will be easier after cooking. Protect your hands while peeling to keep them from turning red!

## Bok Choy

Pick: The darkest-green leaves with firm, pure-white stalks are the best. Brown spots on leaves make this Chinese cabbage less flavorful. Baby bok choy is selected in the same way. As its name implies, it is just a younger cabbage.

Pack: Keep in a plastic bag in the crisper drawer of the fridge for up to three days.

Prep: Separate the stems and rinse. Remove the greens from the stems and cook separately. Baby bok choy can be cooked whole.

## Broccoli

Pick: Choose the head with the tiniest, most compact buds. Broccoli should be dark green with a purply-blue tinge. Avoid broccoli with yellowing buds.

Pack: Store, unwashed, in an open plastic bag in the crisper drawer of the fridge for up to four days.

Prep: Peel away any tough outer skin from the stalk. Rinse in cold water. Cut the stalks and florets to approximately the same size for even cooking.

## Carrots

Pick: Most carrots sold at farmers' markets still have their greens attached, which show the carrots' freshness. Look for bright green leaves. Avoid limp or cracked carrots.

Pack: Remove the leafy green tops before storing, unwashed, in an open plastic bag in the crisper drawer of the fridge for up to six weeks.

Prep: Scrub well to remove dirt and rinse with cold water or simply peel away the outer skin.

## Cauliflower

Pick: Choose firm, creamy white heads with tightly packed florets. The size of the cauliflower doesn't determine its flavor.

Pack: Store, unwashed, stem-side up on a paper towel, in an open plastic bag in the crisper drawer of the fridge for up to five days.

Prep: Remove the outer leaves. Use the cauliflower whole or divide into florets. Cook in stainless steel or enameled cast iron containers to prevent it from turning brown.

## Cherries

Pick: Look for the firmest and plumpest cherries. The freshest cherries are the ones with the greenest stems. Avoid stemless fruit.

Pack: Keep, unwashed, in an open plastic bag in the fridge for up to two days.

Prep: Just before using, rinse in cold water and remove the stems. To remove the pits, use a cherry pitter or paring knife.

## Cucumbers

Pick: Select firm, rich green cucumbers. Usually, smaller cukes have the fewest seeds because they are less mature. Lemon cucumbers should be pale yellow in color and about the size of a baseball.

Pack: Store, unwashed, in a plastic bag in the crisper drawer of the fridge for up to two days.

Prep: Rinse with cold water. If you want to remove the seeds, cut off both ends, slice in half lengthwise, and run the tip of a spoon down the center, scooping up the seeds. Lemon cucumbers usually have tougher skin and so are best peeled.

## Dandelion Greens

Pick: Choose pale green leaves, six inches or less in size, for younger, more tender dandelion greens.

Pack: Rinse repeatedly in cold water until the greens are free of dirt. Shake off excess water, wrap in a paper towel, and store in a plastic bag in the crisper drawer of the fridge for up to four days. The larger the leaf, the longer it will keep.

Prep: Remove tough stems and tear, don't cut, larger leaves to retain the flavor. Smaller leaves can be kept whole. Darker, greener-leaved dandelion greens should be cooked before eating.

## Fava Beans

Pick: Choose fuzzy, bright green pods. Black specks can be normal, but avoid beans with brown spots, which, as with people, are a sign of age. It takes about three pounds of pods to equal one pound of peeled, edible beans.

Pack: Store in a loose plastic bag for up to a week. You can also peel and freeze the beans.

Prep: Shell the beans from the pods immediately before cooking. Blanch the beans in boiling salted water and peel off the light green casings.

## Fresh Herbs

Pick: Choose the freshest-looking herbs, with a heavy scent. Avoid those with limp stems and shriveled ends.

Pack: Store, unwashed, in a plastic bag in the crisper drawer of the fridge for up to a week.

Prep: Rinse just before you are ready to use them. Add them near the end of cooking for the freshest flavor.

## Garlic

Pick: Go for fat, round, firm bulbs with dry, papery skins.

Pack: You'd think vampires would like garlic, because they both like cool, dark places! Store whole heads away from moisture for up to six weeks. Breaking the heads will shorten shelf life. Do not use cloves with green sprouts or brown spots.

Prep: Unless you're roasting the garlic, peel off the skin. Either use a garlic peeler (a rubber tubing device that "rolls" the skin away) or place the flat side of a broad-bladed knife atop a clove and press down firmly with the palm of the hand to remove the skin. To remove skins from large quantities of garlic, place a dozen or more cloves in a bowl. Cover with another bowl to form a sphere and shake vigorously. The skins will fall off.

## Kale

Pick: Choose crisp, firm leaves that are deeply colored without any signs of yellowing. Avoid torn leaves or ones with holes. The smaller the leaf, the more tender and milder in flavor.

Pack: Store the leaves in a plastic bag in the crisper drawer of the fridge for up to three days. The longer they are kept, the more bitter they become.

Prep: Rinse in cool water. Remove the leaf from the center rib and discard the stem.

## Kohlrabi

Pick: When selecting kohlrabi, look to the leaves' freshness. If they are limp or yellowing, choose another! Look for a small to medium size for milder flavor. Bulbs should be firm, without cuts or bruising.

Pack: Remove the leaves from the bulb. Wash the leaves thoroughly in cold water, pat dry, and wrap in a paper towel. Store in a plastic bag in the crisper drawer of the fridge for up to three days. Bulbs should be stored, unwashed, in a plastic bag in the crisper drawer for up to 10 days.

Prep: Smaller bulbs do not need to be peeled, but scrub well under cold water. Larger bulbs should be peeled with a paring knife. Chop the leaves before using.

## Lady Fern Fiddleheads

Pick: Choose tightly closed, bright green coils. Avoid any with black scales.

Pack: Store, unwashed, in plastic wrap in the fridge for up to three days.

Prep: Rub the coils between your palms to remove any brown scales. Rinse under cold water. Trim the stems to one to two inches from the coil.

## Leeks

Pick: Look at the whole leek when choosing. Not only should the top greens be fresh with no yellowing, but the lower portion should be a firm, unblemished white with a pale green color at the base of the leaves. Slightly bend at the pale green section. If it doesn't have a little bend to it, the center has become too tough — choose another! If you're using leeks whole, look for similar-sized ones for even cooking.

Pack: Store, unwashed, in an open plastic bag in the crisper drawer of the fridge for three to five days.

Prep: Cut off the leaves and roots, but not the base. Split the pale green/white section lengthwise, keeping the base intact. Under cold running water, spread the layers apart to remove the dirt that likes to hide among the sections. If slicing for a recipe, place the cut-side down on the cutting surface.

## Lettuce

Pick: Look for lettuces with unwilted leaves and fresh color.

Pack: Wash lettuces before storing. Dry the leaves in a salad spinner or on paper towels. Store in a plastic bag in the crisper drawer of the fridge for five to seven days.

Prep: To avoid bruising, lettuces should be torn, not cut.

### Mustard Greens

Pick: You want fresh-looking, crisp leaves. Avoid yellowing or torn leaves.

Pack: Thoroughly rinse the greens in cold water to make sure you get rid of all dirt. Shake off excess water and wrap in a paper towel. Store in a plastic bag in the fridge for up to three days.

Prep: Remove stems before cooking.

### Peas and Pea Vines

Pick: Look for medium-sized, bright green pods — the peas inside are usually sweeter than those in larger pods. For English peas, shake the pod. If the peas move around easily, pick another pod! Avoid discolored or limp pods. Pea vines (pea shoots) are the leaves at the tips of snow pea stalks. Choose thin tendrils with small, bright leaves that aren't limp or yellowing.

Pack: English pea pods should be refrigerated, unwashed, in a plastic bag in the crisper drawer of the fridge to keep the sugar content from turning to starch. They'll keep for up to two days. Snow peas and sugar snaps are stored in the same way but will last four to seven days. Unwashed pea vines will keep for up to two days in an air-filled plastic bag inside the crisper drawer.

Prep: Rinse with cold water. Most peas will have a string. Snap off the stem and pull the string to the opposite end. For the English peas, pop open and remove the peas from the pod. Discard the stems, keeping leaves and tendrils from pea vines. Rinse in cold water just before using.

### Radicchio

Pick: This chicory "green," although burgundy-red with white in color, comes in head form or a more romaine-like variety. Look for firm heads without signs of wilting or discoloration. Usually, the darker the color, the more bitter the radicchio.

Pack: Store, unwashed, in an open plastic bag in the crisper drawer of the fridge for one to two weeks.

Prep: Remove any discolored outer leaves. To use raw, cut out the center core. Wash the leaves in cold water and pat dry. To cook, you do not need to remove the core — keep whole or cut length-wise into halves or quarters.

### Radishes

Pick: Choose firm radishes without soft spots or cracks. The greens should be bright and crisp.

Pack: Trim the leaves, with about 1/2 inch of stem remaining on the radish. Store unwashed greens in an open plastic bag in the crisper drawer of the fridge for only a couple of days. The roots should be kept the same way but should last up to two weeks.

Prep: Wash under cold water. Pat the leaves dry. Trim the root ends.

### Rapini (broccoli rabe)

Pick: Look for dark green, crisp leaves. Avoid any yellowing.

Pack: Store, unwashed, in an open plastic bag in the crisper drawer of the fridge for up to four days.

Prep: Trim the base of the stalk and remove any wilted leaves.

### Rhubarb

Pick: No matter the color, look for thick (about one inch), firm stalks that are crisp. Avoid blemished stalks and *seriously*, avoid the leaves — if eaten, they can be lethal!

Pack: Wrap unwashed rhubarb in a moist paper towel, place in an open plastic bag, and store in the crisper drawer of the fridge for up to three days.

Prep: Rinse in cold water, then trim the tops and bottoms of the stalks. Peel off any stringy threads (like celery).

### Salad Mix

Pick: There are many to choose from — braising, a Chinese mustard mix, greens with edible flowers, even a spicy salad mix. Ask the farmer for a taste and what each would go best with. No matter which mix you decide on, look for fresh greens.

Pack: Store, unwashed, in an open plastic bag in the crisper drawer of the fridge for up to a week.

Prep: Remove any wilted leaves. Gently wash in cold water and either dry in a salad spinner or pat dry with a paper towel.

### Sea Beans

Pick: These salty specimens should be bright green, without any soft spots or browning.

Pack: Store, unwashed, in a plastic bag in the crisper drawer of the fridge for up to a week. To refresh, soak in iced water for about five minutes.

Prep: Wash with cold water and pat dry. Trim the base of the stems.

### Sorrel

Pick: Choose small, crisp leaves that are bright green in color, without yellowing. Avoid wilted or torn leaves.

Pack: Wrap, unwashed, in a paper towel and store in a plastic bag in the crisper drawer of the fridge for up to three days.

Prep: Thoroughly rinse in cold water. Remove the leaves from the ribs. If chopping the leaves, use a stainless steel knife to avoid discoloration. The smaller-leaved sorrel is more tender, so it can be kept whole. Remove the stems at the base of the leaves.

### Strawberries

Pick: The best market berries are bright and totally red. Look for ones that have no soft spots, discoloration, or mold.

Pack: Unwashed, unhulled berries will keep in the fridge in an airtight container for several days.

Prep: Just before using, wash quickly under cold water. Remove the leaves and stem with the point of a paring knife or a strawberry huller.

### Summer Squash

Pick: Choose firm, unblemished squashes that feel heavy for their size. The smaller the size, usually, the more delicate the flavor.

Pack: Store in plastic bags in the crisper drawer of the fridge for up to four days.

Prep: Simply rinse in cold water — no need to peel.

### Sunchokes

Pick: Choose the smoothest, firmest tubers without discoloration.

Pack: Keep, unwashed, in a plastic bag in the crisper drawer of the fridge for up to a week.

Prep: Since there are many nutrients in the skin, just scrub sunchokes with a brush and dry. If slicing, to prevent them from turning brown, use a stainless steel knife and keep the slices in water with lemon juice for no more than 30 minutes before cooking.

### Watercress

Pick: Choose crisp, dark-green leaves. Usually, the darker the leaves, the better. Leaves should be glossy, not slimy, and should show no signs of yellowing.

Pack: It is best used soon after purchase. Watercress can be kept like a flower bouquet in a jar of water, loosely covered with a plastic bag, in the fridge for only a few days.

Prep: Remove any wilted or bruised leaves. Rinse in cold water, then lightly pat dry. The leaves can be eaten whole, including the stems, or can be torn into pieces.

"GARDENS ARE NOT MADE . . .
BY SITTING IN THE SHADE."

— RUDYARD KIPLING

## FROM THE SOURCE

### PIPITONE FARMS

Owners: Jerry and Andrea Pipitone

Andrea and Jerry Pipitone have adhered to strictly organic practices since 1978, certified first with Tilth Producers, then with the Washington State Department of Agriculture. They own a productive five-acre orchard on the benchland above the Columbia River in the little town of Rock Island. Here the abundant sunshine, the cool waters of the Columbia, and the caring hands of the Pipitones grow wonderful apricots, garlic, Italian plums, nectarines, peaches, peppers, tomatoes, and shallots. Jerry was the 2005 winner of Tilth Producers of Washington's Farm of the Year Award.

"I think it was the publishing of *Silent Spring*, by Rachel Carson, that compelled many of us to take up this way of life. There's a lot of personal satisfaction to what we do. Ninety percent of our customers are seeking organically grown products, and we are sincerely thanked every market day for what we provide." — Jerry Pipitone

# RECIPES

## CARROT SOUP

Serves 4

1 tablespoon olive oil

4 cups chopped carrots (about 7 large, peeled carrots)

1 cup chopped celery (about 3 stalks)

1 cup chopped cucumber (about 1/2 cucumber, peeled and seeded)

1 apple, peeled, cored, and chopped

4 cups vegetable stock

Cucumber, peeled and cut into matchsticks, for garnish

Sound Bites' chimichurri sauce (optional)

Heat the olive oil in a stockpot over medium-low heat. Stir in the carrots, celery, chopped cucumber, and apple. Cover and cook for 20 minutes, or until tender, stirring occasionally.

Remove from the heat. Put 1 cup of stock and one-quarter of the cooked ingredients into a blender and puree. Repeat three times, until all of the stock and vegetables are pureed.

To serve hot, return the soup to the stockpot. Bring to a boil, then reduce the heat and simmer for 10 minutes. To serve cold, store the soup, covered, in the refrigerator until chilled thoroughly.

To garnish, stand cucumber matchsticks in the center of the soup. To add a bit of spice to this soup, add a teaspoon (more if you are daring!) of chimichurri sauce, either stirred in or dolloped on top.

## ENGLISH PEA SOUP WITH MINTED RICOTTA AND MORELS

Chef Holly Smith, Café Juanita, Kirkland

Serves 4

6 cups shelled English peas (best-quality frozen peas can be used)

4-5 ounces (2/3 cup) best-quality chicken stock

5 ounces crème fraîche

1 tablespoon butter, plus more for sautéing morels

Cayenne pepper

Kosher salt

6 ounces whole-milk ricotta

6 mint leaves, finely chopped

4-8 fresh morels, halved if large

Olive oil

Bring a large pot of salted water to a boil. Prepare a large bowl of ice water to shock the peas. Blanch the peas for 45 to 90 seconds, depending on the peas. (Taste at 40 seconds to know!) Plunge the peas into the ice water and swirl around to cool as quickly as possible. This will prevent overcooking and lock in the bright green color. Drain

Reserve 1/4 cup of the blanched peas for the garnish. Puree the remaining peas with enough water to get them going (1/4 cup to start) in a food processor or blender. Strain through as fine a sieve as possible without losing all of the body from the peas. You are hoping to yield 12 ounces (1 1/2 cups) or more of pea puree. If your peas yield less, blanch a few more cups.

Combine the pea puree, chicken stock, crème fraîche, and 1 tablespoon butter in a heavy-bottomed saucepan. Warm gently. When it is just below a simmer, turn the heat down, taste, and add cayenne and kosher salt to taste. Avoid letting this soup boil, as the pea puree may get grainy.

Meanwhile, combine the ricotta with 1/4 teaspoon cayenne pepper and the mint; stir to blend.

Sauté the morels in butter and olive oil over medium-high heat until tender. Season to taste with salt. Keep warm.

Serve the soup in warmed bowls with a sprinkle of the reserved blanched peas, a dollop of ricotta, and a garnish of morels (use as many as you can afford!).

Note: Often I like to sprinkle fruity extra-virgin olive oil over this soup to take it up a notch!

# GRILLED ASPARAGUS WITH HAZELNUT AIGRELETTE AND PINOT NOIR SYRUP

Chef Holly Smith, Café Juanita, Kirkland

Serves 4

## Grilled Asparagus

2 medium bunches local asparagus, tough ends snapped off

3 tablespoons extra-virgin olive oil

Kosher salt

Toss the asparagus in olive oil and salt to taste. Place on a well-heated grill and cook until just tender, 3 to 6 minutes, depending on the heat level.

To serve, arrange the asparagus on a plate. Drizzle Hazelnut Aigrelette (or use a squeeze bottle to make a zigzag) over the asparagus and finish with just a touch of Pinot Noir Syrup as an accent — more aigrelette than syrup. Sprinkle chopped hazelnuts on top.

## Hazelnut Aigrelette (Aioli)

1 shallot, minced

1 tablespoon whole-grain mustard

1 tablespoon fresh lemon juice

3 tablespoons sherry vinegar

2 ounces hazelnut oil

3 ounces extra-virgin olive oil

Salt to taste

4 tablespoons finely chopped toasted hazelnuts (or to taste), divided

Combine the shallot, mustard, lemon juice, vinegar, hazelnut oil, olive oil, and salt in a food processor, or blend vigorously by hand until emulsified. Stir in some of the hazelnuts, reserving some for garnish.

## Pinot Noir Syrup

5 tablespoons organic sugar

1 bottle Pinot Noir (or your favorite red varietal)

In a heavy-bottomed saucepan, melt the sugar over medium heat. When the sugar begins to turn golden, add the wine. Cook down over medium-high heat until syrupy. This should take 10 minutes or so, depending on the heat level. Turn the heat down when the mixture begins to thicken because it goes very quickly from that point on. Let cool and set aside. This is good indefinitely (no need to refrigerate).

## BEET SOUFFLÉ

Serves 4 (as a side dish)

2 tablespoons olive oil, divided

2 medium beets

2 tablespoons butter, plus more for soufflé dish

4 tablespoons grated Parmesan cheese, divided

1 cup beet greens

2 tablespoons flour

3/4 cup chicken broth, heated

1/2 cup grated Gouda cheese

3 eggs yolks, at room temperature

4 egg whites, at room temperature

Preheat the oven to 400°F.

Coat a small roasting pan with 1 tablespoon olive oil. Add the whole, unpeeled beets, cover tightly, and roast for 1 hour, or until tender.

While the beets are roasting, butter a 1-quart soufflé dish and sprinkle with 3 tablespoons grated Parmesan cheese, turning the dish to cover the sides and bottom.

Remove the roasted beets from the oven and let sit, still covered, for 30 minutes. Rub each beet between paper towels to remove the skin. Slice 1/4 inch thick and line the bottom of the soufflé dish with them.

Reduce the oven heat to 350°F.

In a small saucepan, heat 1 tablespoon olive oil over medium heat. Add the beet greens and sauté for just a few minutes, or until wilted. Transfer the beet greens to a board and roughly chop.

In the same pan, melt 2 tablespoons butter over medium heat; stir in the flour. Add the hot chicken broth and cook, stirring continuously, until slightly thickened. Transfer to a larger bowl. Mix in the beet greens and Gouda.

In a separate bowl, beat the egg yolks. Add to the beet greens mixture.

In a mixer bowl, beat the egg whites until soft peaks form. Fold into the greens mixture, blending well. Carefully pour into the soufflé dish. Top with 1 tablespoon Parmesan cheese.

Bake for 30 minutes, or until the soufflé is golden.

## KAI'S TABBOULEH

Kai Ottesen, Hedlin Family Farms, Mount Vernon

Serves 8 to 10

3 cups seasoned or unseasoned bulgur (if seasoned, rinse to remove salt), soaked overnight in 5-6 cups of water

1 cup lemon juice

1/4 cup olive oil

2 cups diced tomatoes (cherry tomatoes work well)

2 cups diced cucumber

2 cups diced bell pepper

2 cups diced sweet onion

1 cup finely chopped fresh parsley

1 cup finely chopped fresh mint

4-5 garlic cloves, crushed

1 cup crumbled feta cheese

Cashews or other nuts, to taste

Mix the bulgur with the lemon juice and olive oil.

Toss the vegetables, herbs, and garlic together and add to the bulgur. Add the feta and nuts and toss.

Let chill in the refrigerator overnight.

## HEDLIN FAMILY FARMS

Owners: Dave Hedlin and Serena Campbell

Hedlin Farms is a century-old family farm located on the outskirts of La Conner. The farm consists of 40 acres of organically grown row crops, 200 acres of seed crops, and 2 acres of hothouses. Their crops include heirloom tomatoes and peppers, spinach, cabbage, cauliflower, and broccoli. Hedlin Farms is serious about conservation and has adopted the philosophy of natural, pesticide-free farming.

# AMERICAN WAGYU TENDERLOIN WITH SOY-MADEIRA GLAZED MUSHROOMS

Chef Aaron Wright, Canlis, Seattle

Serves 4

4  6-ounce fillets of American Wagyu beef tenderloin (or other prime beef tenderloin)

Extra-virgin olive oil

Salt and freshly ground pepper

2 cups Soy-Madeira Glazed Mushrooms (recipe follows)

1/2 cup Port Reduction (recipe follows)

3 cups fresh salad greens

3/4 cup sliced green onions

Before grilling or sautéing the tenderloin, it's important to coat the beef with olive oil. Then season the beef with salt and pepper, and place in a hot pan or on a grill. The oil protects the protein from the heat, preventing the beef from sticking to cooking surfaces as long as the cooking surface is hot. When searing meat in a sauté pan, the thinner the cut of beef, the better. Cook the tenderloin over high heat on both sides to desired doneness.

Place the glazed mushrooms in the center of 4 plates. Drizzle the port reduction around the mushrooms with a spoon. Toss the fresh greens and green onions with olive oil, salt, and pepper to taste, then place on top of the mushrooms. Finish the plates by topping each with a beef tenderloin.

---

## Port Reduction

1 bottle Port wine

Place the Port in a large saucepan and cook over medium-high heat until it is reduced to a glaze. Keep a close eye on the Port once it is reduced to three-quarters of the original volume. When there are lots of shiny bubbles, the glaze is close to finished. Turn the heat down to medium and continue to reduce for a few more minutes. Check the consistency by looking for a steady stream to come off the spoon when pouring. When the reduction pours in an unbroken continuous line, remove from the heat and let the mixture cool to room temperature. This can be stored for up to a month in the refrigerator. Storing sauce in the refrigerator will harden it; let it warm to room temperature before serving.

## Soy-Madeira Glazed Mushrooms

1 pound crimini mushrooms

2 shallots

4 tablespoons extra-virgin olive oil

6 ounces Madeira, cooking grade

2 ounces light soy sauce

Salt and freshly ground pepper

2 tablespoons unsalted butter

Clean the mushrooms with a soft brush and a little water. Trim the stems if necessary. Peel and slice the shallots.

Heat the olive oil in a large sauté pan over medium heat. Add the shallots and mushrooms to the pan and cook, stirring to ensure even browning. When the mushrooms and shallots start to brown, add the Madeira and soy sauce. Allow the liquid to boil and reduce, then taste for seasoning and add salt and pepper if desired. When the liquid is starting to dry up, add the butter to the pan and remove from the heat.

## STEAMED CLAMS WITH SWEET BASIL PESTO

Chef John Howie, Seastar Restaurant and Raw Bar, Bellevue

Serves 4

2 tablespoons extra-virgin olive oil

1 1/2 teaspoons minced garlic

1/2 teaspoon crushed red pepper

1/4 cup clam juice

1/4 cup dry white wine

2 pounds Manila or butter clams, in the shell

1/2 cup Sweet Basil Pesto (see below)

2 tablespoons toasted pine nuts

8 shavings of Parmigiano-Reggiano cheese

Place the olive oil, garlic, and red pepper in a sauté pan over medium heat. Sauté for 1 to 2 minutes, or until the garlic begins to turn golden.

Add the clam juice and wine, stirring to deglaze the pan. When the liquid begins to boil, add the clams. Reduce the heat to low, cover, and cook for 2 to 3 minutes, or until the clams just begin to open.

Add the pesto. Let the mixture cook lightly until the sauce just begins to thicken, then transfer to a heated bowl. Garnish with pine nuts and Parmigiano-Reggiano shavings.

---

**Sweet Basil Pesto**

1/2 cup coarsely chopped fresh basil

1/4 cup coarsely chopped fresh parsley

1 tablespoon minced garlic

1/4 cup toasted pine nuts

1/2 teaspoon kosher salt

3 tablespoons grated Parmigiano-Reggiano cheese

2 tablespoons salted butter

1/3 cup olive oil

Combine the basil, parsley, garlic, pine nuts, salt, and Parmigiano-Reggiano in a food processor. Pulse until finely chopped but not pureed to mush. Add the butter and oil and process to a thick paste.

## PAN-SEARED SALMON AND BING CHERRIES

Chef Aaron Wright, Canlis, Seattle

Serves 4

4 4-ounce skinless
salmon fillets

Salt and pepper

Juice and grated zest of
1/2 lemon

1 teaspoon sugar

1/4 cup plus 2 tablespoons
extra-virgin olive oil, divided

4 mint leaves, sliced thin

1/4 teaspoon pink peppercorns
(optional)

1/2 English cucumber

1 head romaine lettuce

4 ounces Bing cherries

2 ounces goat cheese

Preheat the oven to 450°F.

Season the salmon with salt and pepper to taste; set aside.

In a small bowl, combine the lemon juice, zest, and sugar. Whisk in 1/4 cup olive oil, then add the mint and peppercorns. Add salt and pepper to taste. Set the dressing aside.

Peel the cucumber and slice into thin rounds; place in a salad bowl. Remove the outer leaves from the romaine and add the hearts to the salad bowl (if the romaine is too long, cut into smaller pieces). Add the dressing and mix.

Pit and halve the cherries. Crumble the goat cheese.

Arrange the cucumbers at the base of each serving plate. Place the romaine leaves pointing away from the cucumbers, using them as an anchor. Top the salad with cherries and goat cheese.

Once the plates are set, heat 2 tablespoons olive oil in an ovenproof sauté pan over medium-high heat. When it begins to smoke, add the seasoned salmon to the pan and sear for 2 minutes on each side. Then transfer the pan to the oven for 4 minutes (or to desired doneness). Place the salmon on top of the cucumbers and serve immediately.

## STRAWBERRY-RHUBARB CRUMBLE

Newport High School Culinary Arts class, Bellevue

Serves 8

6 cups hulled and halved strawberries (approximately 2 pounds)

4 1/2 cups rhubarb, trimmed and cut into 1/2-inch pieces

1 1/4 cups sugar

3 tablespoons cornstarch

1 tablespoon fresh lemon juice

1/8 teaspoon salt

1 1/4 cups rolled oats

3/4 cup all-purpose flour

3/4 cup packed light brown sugar

1/4 teaspoon salt

1 1/2 cups unsalted butter, cut into 1/2-inch pieces, slightly softened

Ice cream or whipped cream, for serving

Preheat the oven to 350°F.

Stir together the strawberries, rhubarb, sugar, cornstarch, lemon juice, and salt in a large bowl. Spoon the mixture into a shallow 3-quart baking dish.

Stir together the oats, flour, brown sugar, and salt in a medium-sized bowl. Add the butter and blend with your fingertips until the mixture forms clumps.

Crumble the topping over the filling. Bake until the fruit is bubbling and the topping is golden brown, approximately 40 to 50 minutes.

Cool slightly on a rack and serve warm with ice cream or whipped cream.

## HAYTON FARMS

The Hayton Family

Founded in 1876, Hayton Farms is a fourth- and fifth-generation family farm located halfway between the north and south forks of the Skagit River in Mount Vernon. The first crop was oats, used to feed the horses and also shipped to Seattle. Today, the 200-acre farm produces strawberries, raspberries, blueberries, pickling and slicing cucumbers, cauliflower, peas, and specialty potatoes.

## APRICOT CHEESECAKE

Serves 10 to 12

Nonstick cooking spray

3/4 cup sugar, divided, plus more for dusting the pan

1 pound goat cheese

6 large eggs, separated

1/4 cup flour

1/2 teaspoon almond extract

1/4 teaspoon salt

Apricot Jam (see below)

Preheat the oven to 375°F. Coat a 9-inch springform pan with cooking spray. Sprinkle a few tablespoons of sugar into the pan, coating the bottom and sides. Place the pan in the refrigerator while continuing with the recipe.

In a large bowl, combine the cheese, egg yolks, flour, 6 tablespoons of the sugar, almond extract, and salt. Mix until well blended; set aside.

With an electric mixer, whisk the egg whites on low speed until foamy. Increase the speed to high and gradually add the remaining 6 tablespoons of sugar. Continue mixing until the egg whites form stiff peaks, about 4 minutes.

Fold 1/3 of the egg-white mixture into the cheese mixture until combined. Gently fold in the remaining egg-white mixture until just combined. Pour into the prepared springform pan. Bake in the middle of the oven for about 40 minutes, or until the center is firm and the top is golden brown. To test, insert a skewer into the center; if it comes out clean, the cake is done.

Place the pan on a rack to cool. Remove the cake from the springform pan. Place a plate on top of the cake, invert to remove the pan bottom, then reinvert onto a serving plate. Spread apricot jam over the top of the cheesecake. Serve at room temperature.

### Apricot Jam

1/2 pound apricots, pitted and quartered

1 1/2 teaspoons diced candied ginger

1/4 cup honey

1 tablespoon butter

2 tablespoons lemon juice

Place all ingredients in a heavy saucepan. Simmer over low heat, stirring occasionally, until cooked through and thickened, about 1 1/2 hours. Let cool completely before spreading on the cheesecake.

## PORT MADISON FARM

Owners: Steve and Beverly Phillips

Just across Elliott Bay on Bainbridge Island is the 16-acre Port Madison Farm, where Steve and Beverly Phillips produce yogurt, chèvre, various soft cheeses, and a cheddar, all from pasteurized goat's milk. One hundred Nubian goats live on the farm; 60 of those are milked twice a day, morning and evening. Organic principles are applied at Port Madison Farm; none of the goats are given hormones. Their cheeses are wonderful atop pizza, substituted for ricotta in lasagna, and in cheesecake.

JULY

AUGUST

## MID-SEASON HARVEST

## FROM THE SOURCE: YOUA HER & KAYING'S GARDEN

## RECIPES:

DUTCH ONION SOUP

BROCCOLI ROMANESCO SOUP

RAINBOW CHARD WITH EDAMAME

SUMMER SQUASH BLOSSOM TEMPURA WITH TOMATO AND
PURSLANE SALAD

NIÇOISE SALAD

BELLEVUE FARMERS MARKET RATATOUILLE

RISOTTO WITH SPINACH AND WILD MUSHROOMS

GLAZED PORK TENDERLOIN WITH CUMIN-SPIKED CORN PUREE

WILD SALMON SALAD WITH POMEGRANATE VINAIGRETTE

PEAR POCKET PIES

POACHED TAYBERRY PEARS

CHRISTINA'S HARVEST PEACH PIE

### Asian Pears

Pick: Look for firm, sweet-smelling fruit. If the pear is the yellow-green variety, avoid the more greenish-colored fruit to assure the best taste.

Pack: Store in the fridge for up to three months or at room temperature for about a week.

Prep: Just rinse with cold water and eat!

### Blackberries

Pick: Choose large, plump, sweet-smelling berries that are rich in color with a nice sheen to them. Avoid any with mold. If the berries are runny or extra juicy, they are perfect for jams.

Pack: Go through the container when you get home and pick out any bad berries; one bad one can affect the rest! They are best kept unwashed in a single layer on a paper towel in the fridge for up to three days.

Prep: Lightly rinse with cold water just before serving.

### Blueberries

Pick: Choose plump, firm berries. A whitish bloom on the outside is okay — it helps keep in the moisture of the berry and shows that it wasn't handled too much.

Pack: Sort through the container and pick out any shriveled, squished, or moldy berries. They are best eaten right away but can be kept, unwashed, in an airtight container in the fridge for up to five days.

Prep: Just before using, rinse with cold water and drain.

### Broccoli Romanesco

Pick: With a taste somewhere between broccoli and cauliflower, this vegetable looks prehistoric! Look for tight spirals. Romanesco is chartreuse in color and, unlike regular broccoli, turns a deeper green when cooked.

Pack: Store in an open plastic bag in the crisper drawer of the fridge for up to four days.

Prep: Rinse in cold water. Keep whole and boil for a spectacular presentation or divide into individual spirals.

### Chard (Swiss, rainbow)

Pick: When choosing chard, look at the leaves. Pick the smallest and brightest leaves with no yellowing, holes, or tears. The stems should be unblemished and crisp.

Pack: Keep, unwashed, in a plastic bag in the crisper drawer of the fridge for up to a week. The leaves can be blanched and frozen.

Prep: Wash in cold water. Remove the leaves from the stems. The leaves can be left whole or rolled up and cut into strips. The stems are usually cut diagonally into 1/2-inch slices.

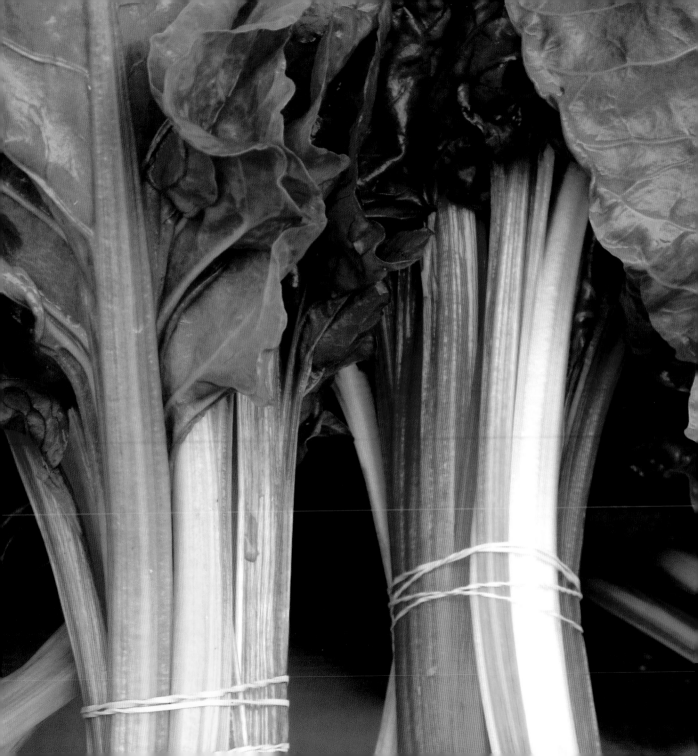

### Collards

Pick: Choose bright-colored leaves. Avoid any with signs of wilting or discoloration.

Pack: Before storing, rinse in cold water to remove all dirt. Shake off excess water, wrap in a paper towel, and store in a plastic bag in the crisper drawer of the fridge for up to three days.

Prep: Remove the stems before cooking.

### Edamame

Pick: These "beans on branches" are soybeans. Look for plump, bright green pods without blemishes.

Pack: Store in an open plastic bag in the crisper drawer of the fridge for up to a week.

Prep: They are best parboiled in the shell in salted water. Drain and pop out the beans from the pods. Use in a recipe or eat edamame on their own, lightly salted.

### Eggplant

Pick: Choose a firm, glossy eggplant that is heavy for its size. Avoid any with soft spots, cuts, or bruises. Small to medium eggplants are best because they are younger.

Pack: Eggplant is best not refrigerated, so store it, unwrapped, in a cool place for up to two days. If you're not using it right away, store in a loose plastic bag in the crisper drawer of the fridge for up to four days.

Prep: Wash in cold water. Remove the cap, using a stainless steel knife to prevent discoloration. To remove excess water before using, lightly salt slices of eggplant on both sides. Lay the slices on paper towels and let sit for 30 to 45 minutes. Rinse with cool water and pat dry.

### Haricots Verts

Pick: These French green beans are thinner and usually a little sweeter than regular green beans. Beans that are about 1/4 inch thick are the most tender.

Pack: Store in an open plastic bag in the crisper drawer of the fridge for up to three days.

Prep: Rinse with cold water. Snap or cut off the ends. Use whole, or if you must cut them, slice on a diagonal. They are so special, they deserve the extra flair!

### Marionberries

Pick: These beautiful purply-black berries look like long blackberries with a tinge of raspberry color. Choose plump berries that are rich in color.

Pack: Once you get them home, pick out any bad-looking berries. They are best kept in a single layer, unwashed, on a paper towel in the fridge for up to three days.

Prep: Lightly rinse with water just before serving.

## Melons

Pick: Choose the melon that has the sweetest smell and a slight softness at the blossom end. Pick one that is heavy for its size. Avoid melons with soft spots, mold, or cracks. If you hear seeds moving around when it is lightly shaken, the fruit is too ripe.

Pack: Ripen, whole, at room temperature. Once it is cut, store in an airtight container in the fridge for up to three days.

Prep: Rinse well with cold water. Cut in half and remove seeds and fibers.

## Nectarines

Pick: I think of this fruit as a shaved peach! Choose as you would a peach: firm but with a little give to it and a sweet smell. Avoid nectarines that have any tinge of green.

Pack: Store at room temperature for up to three days — the fridge will take away some of their flavor. To quicken ripening, store, out of sunlight, in a loosely closed paper bag with an apple or banana. Check daily for ripeness.

Prep: Rinse with cold water. The skin is thin, so there's no need to peel. To remove the pit, slice the fruit in half at the seam. Twist the halves in opposite directions and pull apart.

## Okra

Pick: For the most flavor, pick okra pods that are two to three inches long. Choose crisp pods with moist stem ends. Avoid okra that is blemished or dull-looking.

Pack: Store, unwashed and untrimmed, in a paper bag in the crisper drawer of the fridge for a few days. It's best if used soon after buying.

Prep: Wash with cold water. If using whole, cut off the stem and tip without cutting through to the inside of the pod, to keep the juices inside. When okra is sliced, its stickiness helps to thicken soups. Cook in stainless steel pots to prevent discoloration.

## Onions

Pick: There are many different types of onions: spring, storage, and sweet being their categories. Ask the farmers to describe what varieties they have, and try a new taste each time you visit the market. For spring onions, look for clean stalks and crisp leaves without yellowing. For storage and sweet onions, look for firm onions without soft spots.

Pack: Wrap all partially cut onions tightly in plastic wrap and refrigerate. Store spring onions, unwashed, in an open plastic bag in the crisper drawer of the fridge for up to a week. Store storage and sweet onions, unwashed and not in plastic, in a cool, dry place with good circulation — not the refrigerator. Storage onions should keep for up to two months; sweet onions, up to two weeks. Do not store near potatoes. The onions will absorb moisture from them and will spoil faster.

Prep: To keep from crying while slicing, chill unpeeled onions in the fridge for about an hour before cutting. Also, the farther your eyes are from the onion, the better, so stand while slicing. If all else fails, wear glasses or let someone else slice them for you! To get rid of the onion smell from your hands and cutting surfaces, scrub with lemon juice or vinegar.

## Peaches

Pick: Choose a firm peach that has a little give. No matter what the variety and color, avoid fruit with a greenish undertone because that means it was picked too soon and will never get the best flavor. Avoid peaches with bruises and soft spots. Most important, pick the fruit that has a perfect peach smell.

Pack: Store peaches at room temperature for a few days. To ripen faster, place the fruit in a loosely closed paper bag with an apple or banana. Do not refrigerate peaches unless they are very, very ripe. It's best to use overly ripe peaches in a jam recipe to keep their best flavor, which they can lose if stored in the fridge.

Prep: Rinse with cold water. To shave away the fuzz, gently rub the peach with your fingers under cold water. To remove the pit, slice the peach in half at the seam, then twist the halves in opposite directions.

## Pears

Pick: A good ripe pear will have a little give to it and smell like — big surprise — pear! Avoid pears with bruises or soft spots.

Pack: Eat ripe pears right away. To store unripe pears, keep at room temperature, upright, on the countertop. To quicken ripening, put in a closed paper bag with an apple or banana. When pears are soft near the stem, they are ready! To prolong the life of ripe pears, store in an open plastic bag in the fridge for a few days.

Prep: Rinse in cold water. Peel or keep the skin on, depending on the recipe.

## Plums

Pick: Plums come in different colors, so pick for their richness of color. A whitish bloom is all right — it just means that the fruit has not been handled very much. Select plums that bounce back when you give them a little squeeze.

Pack: Store at room temperature in a single layer to ripen fully. To keep already ripe plums a little longer, refrigerate in an open plastic bag or loosely closed paper bag for up to four days.

Prep: Rinse in cold water. To remove the pit, cut along the seam, twist the halves in opposite directions, and pull apart. The peel can be left on for best flavor.

## Pluots

Pick: Pluots are 75 percent plum/25 percent apricot. Choose plump, firm fruit that gives a little to slight pressure.

Pack: Store unripened pluots in a loosely closed paper bag, away from sunlight. Once they're ripe, store loose in the crisper drawer of the fridge for up to a week.

Prep: Wash with cold water. They can usually be cut all the way through; otherwise, slice along the seam, twist the halves in opposite directions, and pull apart.

## Potatoes

Pick: There are many varieties and different ways to cook them. All fall into a category of either a boiler, a baker (and a candlestick maker?), or an all-purpose potato. In each of these categories there are both new potatoes and storage potatoes. No matter what type of potato, choose firm and unblemished ones that are heavy for their size. Stay away from greenish potatoes or ones that have sprouted or have cuts or cracks. You should be able to rub away the skin of a new potato with your fingers, but not that of a storage potato.

Pack: Store, unwashed, in a paper bag in a cool, dark place. Except for new potatoes, they will keep for a month or longer. Do not store in the refrigerator, which converts the starch to sugar.

Prep: Wash well with cold water. If baking, keep the skins on and prick the potatoes a few times to prevent exploding. If peeling, use a peeler or stainless steel knife to avoid discoloration. If you're not cooking the peeled potatoes right away, submerge them in a bowl of cold water with a few drops of lemon juice to keep the flesh from turning brown.

## Purslane

Pick: Choose succulent leaves without discoloration. This green is very high in omega-3 fatty acids.

Pack: It is best eaten soon after purchase but can be wrapped in a moist paper towel and stored in a plastic bag in the crisper drawer of the fridge.

Prep: Rinse under cold water. Both stems and leaves can be eaten.

## Raspberries

Pick: Yum, raspberries! Look for dark, ruby-red berries that are plump and free of mold.

Pack: Raspberries are best kept at room temperature. Refrigeration takes away some of their delicate flavor. They will keep for two to three days.

Prep: Organic berries do not need washing. Otherwise, quickly rinse with cold water just before using.

## Salad Greens (escarole, frisée)

Pick: Choose crisp leaves with no signs of yellowing.

Pack: Remove any bands or ties around the greens before storing. Place, unwashed, in an open plastic bag in the crisper drawer of the fridge for up to a week.

Prep: Rinse well under cold water to remove any dirt. Dry in a salad spinner or pat dry with a paper towel.

## Spinach

Pick: Choose small, bright green, crisp leaves. Usually the smaller, younger leaves are sweeter. Avoid yellowing.

Pack: Remove the tie holding the leaves together and store, unwashed, in an open plastic bag in the crisper drawer of the fridge for up to three days.

Prep: There can be hidden sand among the leaves, so wash thoroughly, possibly repeatedly, in cold water until all the dirt is gone. Pat dry with a towel or use a salad spinner.

## Squash Blossoms

Pick: Choose the freshest flowers, not limp or wrinkled. Also, pick the brightest-colored blossoms.

Pack: These may last in an open plastic bag in the crisper drawer of the fridge for just a few hours. It's best to use them as soon as you get home from the market.

Prep: Don't wash unless they are very dusty. Check for insects.

## Wild Mushrooms

Pick: Select unblemished, firm mushrooms that are heavy for their size. Avoid ones with tiny holes, which could indicate that there have been bugs present. Mushrooms with open gills should be used as soon as possible.

Pack: Keep, unwashed, in a loosely closed paper bag or on a cookie sheet in a single layer with a moist paper towel on a refrigerator shelf — not in the crisper drawer — for up to a week.

Prep: Most can be wiped clean with a damp paper towel. If they're very dirty, quickly rinse with cold running water and dry thoroughly. For chanterelles and lobster mushrooms, you may need a wet toothbrush to remove grit from the crevices; then pat dry. Reconstitute dried mushrooms in warm water for about 10 minutes.

"EARTH LAUGHS IN FLOWERS."

— RALPH WALDO EMERSON

# FROM THE SOURCE

## YOUA HER & KAYING'S GARDEN

Owner: Pa Yang

Pa Yang came to Washington in 1995 and has continued the Hmong tradition of family farming. Pa and her family grow a beautiful selection of flowers, herbs, and vegetables on a combined 12 acres in Carnation and Monroe. Farming is an important part of the culture for the Hmong, an indigenous people from Southeast Asia. Over the past 25 years, more than 300,000 Hmong have come to this country after being expelled from Laos because of their assistance to the United States during the Vietnam War. During the severe flooding in November 2006, Youa Her & Kaying's Garden were among the many Snoqualmie Valley and Snohomish County farmers who sustained severe damage to their crops.

"It's not an easy life, but I enjoy it because it makes people happy." — Pa Yang

# RECIPES

## DUTCH ONION SOUP

Serves 6

Nonstick cooking spray

3 tablespoons butter,
cut into pieces

4 sweet onions, halved and
cut into 1/4-inch slices

2 red onions, halved and
cut into 1/4-inch slices

1 teaspoon salt

3/4 cup water, divided

6 cups beef broth

1/4 teaspoon ground mace

1 small baguette, cut into
1/2-inch slices

3 cups grated Gouda cheese

Preheat the oven to 400°F.

Coat the inside of a Dutch oven with cooking spray. Place the butter pieces, sliced onions, and salt in the pot. Cover, set in the oven on the lower-middle rack, and cook for 1 hour. Remove from the oven and stir the onions, scraping the bottom and sides of the Dutch oven. Return to the oven with the lid partially covering the pot and continue cooking for 1 hour. Remove from the oven, scrape the sides and bottom again, and return for 45 more minutes with the lid slightly ajar.

Remove the pot from the oven and place on the stovetop over medium heat. Cook, stirring frequently, scraping the sides and especially the bottom, until most of the liquid has evaporated, about 30 minutes. Stir in 1/4 cup of the water, scraping the bottom to remove the crust, and cook for about 5 minutes, or until the liquid has evaporated and the bottom of the pan has crusted again. Repeat this process two more times. The onions will be a beautiful dark brown color.

Stir in the beef broth and mace. Scrape away any final bits of crust from the sides and bottom of the Dutch oven. Increase the heat to high, bringing it just to a boil. Then reduce the heat to low and simmer for 30 minutes.

While the soup is simmering, place the baguette slices on a baking sheet in a single layer. Bake for 5 minutes on each side, or until the bread is crisp and golden. Remove from the oven and set aside.

Position the oven rack 6 inches from the broiler. Heat the broiler on low.

Set 6 individual ovenproof serving bowls on a baking sheet. Fill each bowl with about 1 1/2 cups of soup. Top with baguette slices, not overlapping, and sprinkle with 1/2 cup of grated Gouda. Broil until the cheese has melted, about 3 minutes. Let cool for about 5 minutes before serving.

## GOLDEN GLEN CREAMERY

Owners: Judy Jensen, Brandy Jensen, and Andrea Jensen

The Creamery is woman-owned and -operated, and has been making cheese since mid-August 2004. All of the cheese is handmade, with only the ingredients that were intended to be there: milk, cultures, vegetable rennet, salt, and some spices here and there. The milk that is used to make the cheeses is produced on-site by Vic Jensen & Sons Dairy.

## BROCCOLI ROMANESCO SOUP

Serves 8

2 pounds broccoli Romanesco

1/4 cup olive oil

1/2 cup diced onion

1/2 cup chopped celery

1/2 cup chopped leek (white and light green part)

1/4 cup flour

6 cups chicken broth

1/2 cup heavy cream, heated

1 tablespoon fresh lemon juice

Salt and pepper

Grated nutmeg, a pinch for each bowl

Trim off the base of the broccoli so you are left with separate spirals and stems. Set aside 1 cup of spirals for garnish. Chop the remaining spirals and stems.

Heat the olive oil in a large stockpot over medium heat. Add the onion, celery, leek, and broccoli. Cook, stirring frequently, for 8 to 10 minutes.

Add the flour and continue cooking and stirring for another 3 minutes. Gradually add the chicken broth, whisking to remove any lumps of flour. Bring to a simmer and cook for 25 minutes, stirring frequently and skimming off fat, if needed.

Working in batches, puree the soup until it is as smooth as heavy cream. Return the soup to the pot and simmer over low heat.

Blanch the reserved broccoli spirals in boiling water until tender.

Remove the soup from the heat and add the heated cream. Stir in the lemon juice. Season to taste with salt and pepper.

Serve in individual bowls, placing a few broccoli spirals in the center of each bowl and sprinkling with a pinch of nutmeg.

## RAINBOW CHARD WITH EDAMAME

Serves 4 (as a side dish)

2 pounds rainbow chard

1 cup shelled edamame

1 1/2 tablespoons olive oil, divided

1/4 teaspoon salt, plus more to taste

1/8 teaspoon freshly ground black pepper, plus more to taste

2 teaspoons chopped fresh oregano

1 teaspoon lemon juice

Remove the leaves from the stems and center rib of the chard. Reserve the leaves for another recipe. Cut the stems in half, on the diagonal. Have a large bowl of ice water ready for the blanched vegetables.

In a large stockpot, bring 4 quarts of salted water to a boil. Add the chard stems and blanch for 3 minutes. Remove with a slotted spoon and immediately immerse in the ice bath. Transfer to a towel to drain. Repeat the process with the edamame, also blanching for 3 minutes.

Preheat the broiler to high.

Toss the chard stems with 1 tablespoon olive oil, salt, and pepper. Place on a broiler pan and broil for 2 minutes on each side, or until slightly browned.

Heat the remaining olive oil (1 1/2 teaspoons) in a large skillet over medium-low heat. Stir in the oregano, then add the chard and edamame. Cook, stirring, for 2 minutes. Pour the lemon juice over the top and toss. Add salt and pepper to taste.

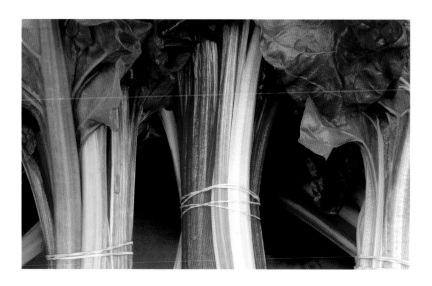

## SUMMER SQUASH BLOSSOM TEMPURA WITH TOMATO AND PURSLANE SALAD

Chef Kelly Gaddis, (formerly) Porcella Urban Market, Bellevue

Serves 4

### Tempura Blossoms

1/2 cup fresh chèvre, softened to room temperature

2 eggs

2 tablespoons chopped fresh soft herbs such as basil, marjoram, or parsley

4 large summer squash blossoms with no frazzled flower tips

1 cup flour, plus more for dusting

1 cup water

Pinch of salt

4 cups peanut oil

1 small summer onion, sliced into thin rings, for garnish

In a mixing bowl, combine the chèvre, 1 egg, and the herbs. Place the mixture in a pastry bag or a resealable plastic bag with the bottom corner cut off. Gently open each squash blossom. Holding the flower in one hand, insert the pastry bag tip into the flower and squeeze until it fills the flower. Carefully twist the blossom closed. Refrigerate for at least 1 hour.

Place 1 cup flour in a medium mixing bowl. Stirring with a whisk, add 1 egg, the water, and salt. Set aside.

*Fresh Chevre*

*Hand made from Grade A pasteurized goat milk, culture, enzymes and salt.*

**Salad**

1/2 teaspoon honey

2 pinches truffle salt

1 teaspoon chopped fresh
thyme leaves

1 teaspoon chopped black
truffle, fresh or canned

1 tablespoon finely
diced shallot

1/2 cup champagne vinegar

1/2 cup olive oil

Salt and pepper

4 heirloom tomatoes of
varying sizes

1 bunch purslane, cleaned
and trimmed, or you can
substitute mâche, sorrel, or
other small-leaved salad green

1/2 head of baby frisée,
washed and picked

Nigella seeds, for garnish

Basil oil, for garnish

To prepare the salad, combine the honey, truffle salt, thyme, chopped truffle, and shallot with vinegar in a medium mixing bowl. Briskly whisk in the olive oil. Check for seasoning, and add salt and pepper to taste. Set aside.

Cut the tomatoes into wedges, 12 for large tomatoes, 8 for medium, 2 for small pears, and so on.

**Final Preparation**

Heat the peanut oil to 350°F in a small, high-rimmed sauce pot with enough room for the flowers.

Toss the squash blossoms in a bowl with the remaining "dusting" flour. Dip into the batter, put into the hot oil, and fry until the batter is crisp, keeping an eye on them to make sure they don't get too dark. Remove with a slotted spoon and set aside on a paper towel. Now, do the same with the sliced onions.

To assemble the salad, place the tomatoes, purslane, and frisée in a large bowl and toss with the champagne vinaigrette.

Arrange wedges of each type of tomato on chilled plates, place a few greens on top, and nestle a squash blossom up against the salad. Garnish with nigella seeds, basil oil, and onions.

## NIÇOISE SALAD

Serves 8

3/4 pound haricots verts, topped and tailed and blanched

1 pound white new potatoes, cooked and quartered

1 pound red new potatoes, cooked and quartered

6 small tomatoes, quartered

1 head of butter lettuce

1 package (1 pound) St. Jude's smoked tuna

6 hard-boiled eggs, peeled and quartered

1/2 pound black olives, pitted

2 tablespoons capers, drained

························································

### Dressing

3 tablespoons champagne vinegar

1 tablespoon Dijon mustard

1/2 teaspoon salt

1/4 teaspoon freshly ground black pepper

10 tablespoons olive oil

To prepare the dressing, combine the vinegar, mustard, salt, and pepper in a small jar. Tightly close the lid and shake. Add the olive oil, replace the lid, and shake until emulsified.

In three separate bowls, mix a small amount of the dressing with the haricots verts, potatoes, and tomatoes.

Line a large platter with the lettuce. Arrange the haricots verts, potatoes, tomatoes, tuna, and eggs on the lettuce. Sprinkle with the olives and capers. Serve the remaining dressing on the side in a pitcher.

## FISHING VESSEL *ST. JUDE*

Owners: Joe and Joyce Malley

The Malleys are a family business based in Seattle. Joe Malley started out salmon trolling in Sitka, Alaska, in 1978. From there he moved into longlining, pursuing halibut, black cod, and Pacific cod around the Gulf of Alaska. Presently, Joe owns the fishing vessel *St. Jude*, which trolls solely for albacore tuna in the North and South Pacific. The Malleys' tuna is low in mercury and high in omega-3 oils, and is caught in a sustainable manner.

# BELLEVUE FARMERS MARKET RATATOUILLE

Chef J.J. Johnson, private chef, Seattle

Serves 6

1 tablespoon vegetable oil

1 small sweet onion, cut in 1/4-inch dice

1 garlic clove, minced

1 very small pinch crushed red pepper

1 small fennel bulb, cut in 1/4-inch dice

1 small white, graffiti, or Asian (Japanese/Chinese/Thai) eggplant, cut in 1/4-inch dice

1 red bell pepper, cut in 1/4-inch dice

1 small zucchini, cut in 1/4-inch dice

1 or 2 medium ripe tomatoes, seeded and cut in 1/4-inch dice

3 tablespoons chopped fresh herbs, such as basil, parsley, tarragon, or marjoram

White balsamic vinegar, to taste

Extra-virgin olive oil, to taste

Sea salt and freshly ground black pepper, to taste

In a large nonreactive skillet, heat the vegetable oil over medium heat. Add the onions, garlic, and crushed red pepper. Sauté for approximately 2 to 3 minutes, stirring frequently.

Add the remaining vegetables in the order listed, cooking each for about 2 minutes before adding the next. When the tomatoes are lightly cooked but not mushy, add the herbs, vinegar, and olive oil. Season well with salt and pepper.

Let the ratatouille cool slightly, then serve with grilled fish or meat, fresh penne pasta, or bruschetta. Any leftovers reheat very well in a sauté pan in about 2 minutes. Ratatouille is also great at room temperature.

# RISOTTO WITH SPINACH AND WILD MUSHROOMS

Chef John Howie, Seastar Restaurant and Raw Bar, Bellevue

Serves 4

2 tablespoons extra-virgin olive oil

1 tablespoon minced shallots

2 teaspoons minced garlic

1/4 cup minced fresh leeks, white and light green part only

1/2 pound Arborio rice

1 1/2 cups dry white wine

4 cups vegetable stock

4 tablespoons butter

1 1/2 cups wild mushrooms cut into 1/4-inch slices (porcini, chanterelles, or others)

3/4 cup heavy cream

2 teaspoons chopped fresh basil leaves, plus 4 sprigs for garnish

2 cups baby spinach

1 teaspoon sea salt

1/2 teaspoon freshly ground black pepper

1/4 cup grated Parmigiano-Reggiano cheese

Heat the olive oil in a heavy-gauge saucepot over medium-high heat. Add the shallots, garlic, and leeks. Sauté for about 1 minute, but don't brown. Add the rice and continue to sauté, stirring, until the rice is well coated. Add the wine and let reduce until the liquid is almost gone.

Lower the heat and bring to a simmer. Add the vegetable stock 1 cup at a time and simmer, working the ingredients with a rubber spatula, until the liquid is almost gone before adding the next cup. Continue to follow this procedure until the rice is al dente and a creamy, medium-thick consistency is achieved. When making risotto, sometimes you need less stock and sometimes you need more. This will be based on how quickly you evaporate the liquid in the pan. Add or delete stock as necessary to ensure that the rice is creamy but is still slightly al dente before adding the rest of the ingredients.

Meanwhile, melt the butter in a sauté pan over medium heat. Add the mushrooms and slowly sauté until tender. Add the sautéed mushrooms to the al dente risotto.

Then stir in the cream, chopped basil, spinach, salt, pepper, and Parmigiano-Reggiano. When the spinach is wilted, add stock if needed to make it creamy. Divide evenly among pasta bowls. Garnish with the basil sprigs and serve immediately.

Note: Risotto takes patience to cook. If you try to do it too quickly, you will end up with sticky rice with a crispy center. Slow cookery is the best for risotto. Your risotto will be creamy and tender, with a slight bite to the tooth!

## GLAZED PORK TENDERLOIN WITH CUMIN-SPIKED CORN PUREE

Chef Emmanuel Piqueras, (formerly) Mixtura, Kirkland

Serves 4 to 6

3 large tomatillos or 1/2 pound Cape gooseberries, husked and chopped

3 jalapeños, seeded and chopped

2 scallions, chopped

1/2 teaspoon chopped fresh rosemary

4 garlic cloves, minced, divided

7 tablespoons extra-virgin olive oil, divided

1 tablespoon plus 1 teaspoon honey, divided

2  1-pound pork tenderloins

Piqueras sampled a suckling pig dish in the Andean village of Huarocondo, which inspired this tangy, slightly sweet and spicy pork tenderloin recipe. Cape gooseberries or tomatillos replace the original sour green tomatoes, and pisco stands in for the fermented corn alcohol *chicha de jora*.

In a food processor, puree the tomatillos with the jalapeños, scallions, rosemary, 1 garlic clove, 2 tablespoons olive oil, and 1 tablespoon honey. Pour the puree into a large, sturdy resealable plastic bag. Add the pork tenderloins, coat well, and refrigerate overnight.

In a medium saucepan of boiling water, cook the corn until just tender, about 3 minutes; drain. In a food processor, puree the corn with the yellow pepper.

In a medium skillet, heat 2 tablespoons of the olive oil. Add the onion, ham, and remaining garlic and cook over moderate heat until the onion is softened, about 7 minutes. Add 2 tablespoons of the pisco and light carefully with a long match. When the flames die down, add the corn and pepper puree and 1 cup of the stock and simmer over low heat for 15 minutes, stirring occasionally. Add the parsley and cumin and season to taste with salt and pepper. Cover and set aside.

Remove the pork tenderloins from the marinade; reserve the marinade. In a large skillet, heat the remaining 3 tablespoons of olive oil over moderate heat. Season the tenderloins with salt and pepper, add them to the skillet, and cook until browned on all sides, about 1 minute per side. Add the remaining 1/4 cup of pisco and light carefully. When the flames die down, add the reserved marinade and the remaining 1 1/2 cups of stock and bring to a boil. Cover and simmer over moderately low heat, turning occasionally, until the pork is pink in the center, about 20 minutes.

3 cups fresh corn kernels
(from 6 ears of corn)

1/2 yellow bell pepper, chopped

1 medium red onion, cut into
1/3-inch dice

1/4 pound smoked ham, cut
into 1/3-inch dice

1/4 cup plus 2 tablespoons pisco
(South American brandy), or
other brandy, divided

2 1/2 cups vegetable stock

2 tablespoons chopped
fresh parsley

1/4 teaspoon ground cumin

Salt and pepper

Transfer the pork to a carving board and cover loosely with foil. Boil the pan sauce over moderately high heat for 3 minutes. Set a fine sieve over a small saucepan and strain the sauce, pressing on the solids. Add the remaining 1 teaspoon of honey and season to taste with salt and pepper.

Gently reheat the corn puree. Thickly slice the pork and transfer to plates. Pour the sauce over the pork, spoon the corn puree alongside, and serve.

# WILD SALMON SALAD WITH POMEGRANATE VINAIGRETTE

Chef Dan Thiessen, 0/8 Seafood Grill, Bellevue

Serves 4

4 ounces pomegranate juice

1 ounce cider vinegar

3 ounces canola oil, divided

2 tablespoons minced garlic

1 tablespoon minced shallot

4  6-ounce wild salmon fillets

Sea salt and black pepper

8 cups assorted salad greens

2 cups assorted fresh berries

Combine the pomegranate juice, vinegar, 2 ounces canola oil, garlic, and shallots for the vinaigrette.

Heat a large sauté pan with the remaining 1 ounce canola oil over medium-high heat until the oil shimmers in the pan. Season the salmon with sea salt and pepper to taste, and sear in the pan on both sides until golden brown.

Place the greens and berries in a salad bowl and toss with the vinaigrette.

Arrange the salad on plates and top with the seared salmon.

## PEAR POCKET PIES

Chef Jenny Christensen, Pies by Jenny, Seattle

Makes 4 individual pies

6 cups water

3 cups sugar

4 rosemary sprigs

4 tablespoons lemon juice

2 pears

Parchment paper

4 tablespoons blue cheese

1 egg

4 teaspoons turbinado sugar

**Pie Dough**

2 1/2 cups flour

1 teaspoon salt

2 sticks unsalted butter,
cut into very small pieces

1/3 cup cold water

To prepare the pie dough, have all ingredients very cold before beginning. Whisk together the flour and salt in a large bowl. Cut in the butter pieces with a pastry blender or by hand until the mixture looks like coarse crumbs. Add the water in small amounts, stirring into the flour mixture until the dough holds together without being sticky. If the dough is crumbly when you squeeze a small amount together, add water a tablespoon at a time. Divide the dough in half and place on a piece of plastic wrap. Flatten into round disks, wrap in plastic, and refrigerate for at least 1 hour or overnight.

Preheat the oven to 425°F.

Place the water and sugar in a large stockpot and bring to a boil. Reduce the heat and simmer until the sugar is dissolved. Add the rosemary sprigs and lemon juice.

Peel, halve, and core the pears and quickly place in the simple syrup to avoid discoloration. Turn off the heat. Cover the pears with parchment paper and place a small plate on top to keep the pears submerged. Let sit for about 30 minutes, or until the pears are tender.

Remove the pears from the stockpot. Fill the cavity of each pear half with 1 tablespoon of blue cheese.

Roll out 1 disk of dough to approximately a 10-inch circle. Slice down the middle to divide the dough in half. Lay a pear half on a piece of pastry, with the stem end at the top edge. Fold up the bottom of the dough over the pear and form over the pear, cutting off excess dough. Press or crimp the edges to seal. Repeat for the remaining pastry and pears. You can make leaves or other designs with the leftover dough for decoration.

Place the pear pies on a parchment-covered baking sheet. Whisk together the egg and 1 tablespoon of water. Brush the egg wash over the pies and sprinkle each with 1 teaspoon of turbinado sugar.

Bake for 10 minutes. Reduce the heat to 350°F and continue baking for 30 minutes, or until golden.

## POACHED TAYBERRY PEARS

Wade Bennett, Rockridge Orchards & Cidery, Enumclaw

Serves 4

4 Bosc pears

1/2 cup crystalized ginger, diced

Rockridge Orchards tayberry wine

1 tablespoon butter

Preheat the oven to 200°F.

Pare the pears! Core from the bottom to about 1/2 inch from the stem. Trim the bottom so the pear sits flat.

Fill the core cavity of each pear with diced ginger. Place the pears, standing upright, in an ovenproof enamel-bottomed pot. Pour enough tayberry wine into the pot to go one-quarter of the way up the sides of the pears. Carefully cover with a lid or foil.

Bake for 2 hours. Then carefully remove the lid and baste the pears with the pan liquid. Cover and continue baking for 15 minutes. Baste the pears one more time and bake 15 minutes longer, or until just tender.

Place the pears in a separate bowl to cool. Add the butter to the wine sauce and set over high heat on the stove to reduce, stirring constantly until it thickens enough to coat the back of the spoon. Watch carefully — the sauce will quickly turn from the perfect thickness to a perfect nightmare! Remove from the heat immediately.

To serve, place each pear on an individual serving dish. Pour the wine sauce over the pears. These also taste great the next day. Refrigerate the pears and sauce separately. Before serving, brush some of the sauce onto the pears with a pastry brush, then place the pears in individual serving dishes and top with sauce.

## ROCKRIDGE ORCHARDS & CIDERY

Owners: Wade and Judy Bennett

Rockridge Orchards was started in 1991 as a small farm employing family, friends, and neighbors. They produce over 148 different crops, including heirloom tomatoes, cucumbers, pears, apples, and raspberries, and specialize in "exotic edibles" such as bamboo shoots, toonie, fuki, wasabe, yuzu, sansho, hardy ginger, and bananas — to name just a few!

## CHRISTINA'S HARVEST PEACH PIE

Christina Dudley, contributor/writer for *Market Fresh* newsletter, Bellevue

Serves 8

2 pounds peaches

2/3-3/4 cup packed light brown sugar (use lesser amount if peaches are sweet)

1/3 cup flour

1 tablespoon lemon juice

1/2 teaspoon ground cinnamon

1/8 teaspoon grated nutmeg

Handful of blueberries or raspberries

1/2 recipe Joyce's Never-Fail Pie Crust (see below)

Milk

Preheat the oven to 425°F.

Bring a large pot of water to a boil. Add the peaches for about 30 seconds. Remove with a slotted spoon and place on a towel to drain. The skins should just slip off. Pit the peaches and slice thickly.

In a large bowl, mix the peaches with the brown sugar, flour, lemon juice, cinnamon, nutmeg, and berries.

Line a 9-inch pie pan with a bottom crust. Pour in the filling and top with the second crust, pinching the edges together to seal. Cut ventilation slits in the top. Brush the crust with a little milk.

Place the pie on a rimmed baking sheet and bake for 40 to 50 minutes, or until the crust is golden brown and the filling is bubbling. Let cool on a rack.

## JOYCE'S NEVER-FAIL PIE CRUST

Joyce Bloomquist, choir member, First Presbyterian Church, Bellevue

3 cups flour

1 teaspoon salt

1 1/4 cups shortening

1 egg

1 tablespoon white vinegar

5 tablespoons water

Mix the flour and salt in a large bowl. Cut in the shortening until the mixture makes fairly uniform "pebbles."

Mix the wet ingredients in a small bowl and add, 2 tablespoons at a time, to the dry mixture, blending with a fork.

Divide into 4 portions. (If you're making only one pie, wrap 2 portions in plastic wrap and freeze for later use.) Roll out for crust.

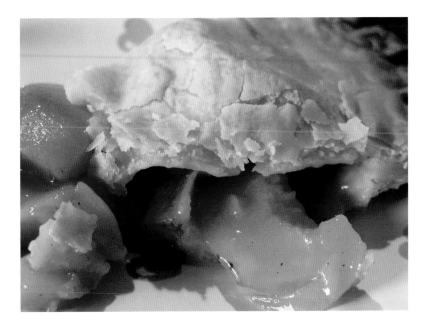

# SEPTEMBER
# OCTOBER

## LATE-SEASON HARVEST

## FROM THE SOURCE: KITTITAS VALLEY GREENHOUSE

## RECIPES:

WINTER SQUASH SOUP

HEIRLOOM TANDEM TOMATO SOUP

SWEET CORN AND CHERRY TOMATO SALAD

LOBSTER MUSHROOMS WITH FENNEL AND TOMATO

PARSNIP, TURNIP, AND CELERIAC PATTIES WITH TOMATILLO SALSA

MUSSELS PROVENÇAL

COCOA NIB CRUSTED LAMB LOINS

GINGER POT ROAST WITH VEGETABLES AND STAR ANISE

SUGAR PIE PUMPKIN PIE

SNAPPY APPLE TART

## Apples

Pick: To enjoy a nice crisp, juicy apple, choose one that is firm, with a smooth skin. Avoid fruit with bruises, soft spots, or holes.

Pack: Apples continue to ripen once picked, so eat them quickly if keeping at room temperature. Keep in a cool, dark place, or best, store in a plastic bag in the crisper drawer of the fridge for up to six weeks.

Prep: Rinse with cold water and enjoy. Unless a recipe calls for peeled apples, it's best to keep their skins on to get the most nutrients.

## Artichokes

Pick: Since the globe artichoke is the unopened flower bud of a plant from the thistle family, choose the bud that is tightly closed. Pick one that feels heavy for its size and is mostly green. Brown-colored streaks are only frost marks, which sometimes sweeten the artichoke. Do not select those with black streaks.

Pack: If the artichoke has a long-enough stalk, place the stem end in water and refrigerate. Otherwise, store, unwashed and uncut, in an open plastic bag in the crisper drawer of the fridge for up to a week.

Prep: Wash in cold water. Twist off the stalk, which removes some of the fibers from the base. Using a stainless steel knife, even off the base. Trim the tops off the thorny leaves with scissors and squeeze lemon juice over the cut areas to prevent discoloration.

## Cabbage

Pick: Choose large, tight heads with bright, crisp leaves. Pick cabbages that are heavy for their size, without cuts or bruises.

Pack: The firmer the cabbage, the longer it will keep. Green cabbage should be used within a few days if eaten raw. Otherwise, store, unwashed and uncut, in an open plastic bag in the crisper drawer of the fridge for up to two weeks. Savoy cabbage will last in the fridge for only about four days. Red cabbage will last in the fridge for about a week.

Prep: Remove wilted leaves and rinse under cold water. Cut out the core. With red cabbage, cut with a stainless steel knife to avoid discoloration and cook with vinegar or other acidic ingredient to keep it from turning blue-gray in color.

## Celery

Pick: Choose shiny, light green celery that is heavy for its size. Darker-green bunches can be stringy. Avoid stalks that are bruised or have yellowing leaves.

Pack: Trim off the base of the celery, remove any damaged bits, and store, unwashed, in a plastic bag in the crisper drawer of the fridge for up to two weeks. To bring limp celery back to life, wrap it in a moist paper towel and place, leaf end up, in a glass of cold water.

Prep: Separate the stalks and rinse well with cold water to remove any hidden dirt. Peel away the strings from tough outer stalks with a vegetable peeler. The leafy tops can be chopped into salads or used to flavor soups.

## Corn

Pick: The freshest corn has a moist, pale green stem. Look for plump corn with tight, bright-green husks with dark silk sprouting out the top. If you are allowed to push at a kernel, a milky juice will seep out of a fresh ear.

Pack: Best to eat it the day you buy it, but if you must . . . to keep moisture in the corn, store unhusked in a plastic bag in the coldest part of the fridge no longer than two days. If the ears are already husked or partially husked, store in an open plastic bag in the crisper drawer of the fridge.

Prep: Remove the husks ("shuck the corn") and silks. You can leave the husks on when grilling or roasting.

## Figs

Pick: Choose figs that have a bit of resistance when lightly pressed, but are soft to the touch — not hard.

Pack: Keep at room temperature for up to three days. To hold them a little longer, place on a plate in a single layer, cover with a paper towel and then plastic wrap, and store in the fridge for up to a week.

Prep: Trim off the stem and rinse under cold water. Gently pat dry.

## Grapes

Pick: Grapes don't continue to ripen after being picked, so look for firm, round, fragrant grapes. A powdery finish, or bloom, is a sign of freshness and of not being handled too much. Green grapes should have a golden hue, while darker grapes will have a deep tone.

Pack: Pick off any bad grapes in the bunch and store, unwashed, in an open plastic bag in the crisper drawer of the fridge for up to 10 days. For a tasty treat on a hot summer day, wash grapes, carefully pat dry, put in a plastic bag, and freeze. Eat straight out of the freezer!

Prep: They're best served at room temperature, so take them out of the fridge about an hour before eating. Rinse with cool water.

### Parsnips

Pick: Choose small to medium-sized parsnips that are firm and blemish free. Usually the whiter the parsnip, the more tender.

Pack: Store in an open plastic bag in the crisper drawer of the fridge for up to three weeks.

Prep: Scrub well under cold water or peel the outer skin with a vegetable peeler.

### Peppers

Pick: There are many to choose from — either sweet in flavor or fiery hot. Ask the farmer about the many varieties. Look for a pepper that is firm, is heavy for its size, and has a fresh, green stem. Avoid any with soft spots or cracks. All peppers start out green and ripen to yellow, orange, red — whatever the variety.

Pack: For sweet peppers, store, unwashed, in a plastic bag in the crisper drawer of the fridge for up to a week. For hot peppers, store, unwashed, in a paper bag in the crisper drawer for up to a week.

Prep: Wash under cold water. Core and remove seeds. When handling chile peppers, always wear gloves to protect your hands from spreading the heat, and wash your hands and nails thoroughly afterward.

### Tomatillos

Pick: Choose this fresh-tasting non-relative of the tomato by its firmness. Pick fruit that fills out the husk. Do not pick ones that are out of their husks.

Pack: Store loose in the crisper drawer of the fridge for up to two weeks.

Prep: Peel the husks. Rinse the tomatillos with cold water, removing stickiness. Pat dry with a paper towel.

### Tomatoes

Pick: There are many different colors and tastes. Smell the fruit and choose ones with a great tomatoey aroma. Look for plump, firm tomatoes that are heavy for their size.

Pack: Never refrigerate tomatoes. Keep at room temperature, away from sunlight, for up to a week. Eat them as soon as they are ripe!

Prep: Wash in cold water. Tomatoes can be prepared in many ways, so follow the recipe to decide whether you need to peel, core, or deseed.

## Turnips

Pick: The greens of these little "tops" will show the turnip's freshness, so look for fresh greens. Pick the smallest of this root vegetable — usually the sweetest — but also pick the ones that feel heavy for their size. Choose firm turnips with unblemished skins.

Pack: Remove the greens from the roots and store separately, unwashed, in an open plastic bag in the crisper drawer of the fridge for up to a week.

Prep: Scrub under cold water. Small turnips can be eaten with the peel on. Peel the outer layer of skin of bigger roots with a paring knife.

## Wild Huckleberries

Pick: Huckleberries at the market are such a treat, you should grab whatever they have before they are gone. You will find the dark purply-blue, ripe berries ready to go home with you!

Pack: If you don't eat them right away, they can be stored in the refrigerator for up to two days.

Prep: Rinse if you must, but you will also rinse away the wonderful juices; just pick out any bad ones and gobble 'em up!

## Winter Squash/Pumpkins

Pick: When selecting a pumpkin for ornamental use, I choose the ugliest one because I know no one else will! However, when you're planning to eat it, go for the heaviest, for the most flesh. Choose a hard squash with no cracks, bruises, or mold.

Pack: Uncut, winter squash will keep in a cool, dark, well-ventilated spot for months. Once it is cut, store in plastic wrap in the fridge. Cooked and pureed, it will keep in the freezer for up to three months.

Prep: Scrub the outside before cooking. The skin is so hard, it is best to carefully slice in half, remove seeds and strings, and bake.

## Yu Choy

Pick: Look for bright green leaves and crisp stalks.

Pack: It will keep in a plastic bag in the crisper drawer of the fridge for up to five days.

Prep: Trim a bit off the ends of the stems. Rinse in cold water. Remove leaves from the stalk. Chop the leaves and cut the stems into 1/2-inch slices.

"ALL THE FLOWERS OF ALL THE TOMORROWS ARE IN THE SEEDS OF TODAY."

— INDIAN PROVERB

# FROM THE SOURCE

## KITTITAS VALLEY GREENHOUSE

Owners: Richard Ness and Mary Young-Ness

Richard and Mary started Kittitas Valley Greenhouse in 1988. They grow the highest-quality hydroponic tomatoes, which means that the plants are grown using mineral solutions and without soil. The greenhouse utilizes its own natural and pure spring water. There are no trace pesticides or herbicides in the spring water, and even in water-short years, there is sufficient water for the greenhouse to yield crops from May through November. Kittitas Valley Greenhouse specializes in growing heirloom tomato varieties that are not found in many other places in the area.

# RECITES

## WINTER SQUASH SOUP

Chef Brian Scheehser, Trellis, Kirkland

Serves 6

2 medium-small winter squashes (yielding 2 1/2 cups cooked squash)

1 shallot, chopped

1 carrot, chopped

1 leek, white part only, washed and chopped

1 small yellow onion, chopped

2 celery stalks, chopped

2 tablespoons olive oil

3 thyme sprigs

1 bay leaf

6 1/2 cups chicken stock

1 pound russet potatoes (about 3), washed and chopped

Salt and pepper

Preheat the oven to 350°F.

Scrub the squashes. Cut in half and scoop out the seeds. Discard the seeds. Place cut-side down on a rimmed baking sheet. Add water to cover the bottom of the baking sheet. Bake until completely soft, about 1 hour. Scoop the flesh from the shells to obtain approximately 2 1/2 cups cooked squash. Set aside.

In a large stockpot, sweat the shallots, carrots, leeks, onions, and celery in olive oil over very low heat until soft and translucent. Tie the thyme sprigs and bay leaf in cheesecloth and add to the stockpot with the cooked squash, chicken stock, and potatoes. Simmer over low heat until the potatoes are soft. Remove from the heat and discard the packet of herbs.

Working in batches, transfer to a food processor or blender and process until smooth. Add salt and pepper to taste. Serve hot.

# HEIRLOOM TANDEM TOMATO SOUP

Serves 6 to 8

## Tomato Basil Soup

2 tablespoons olive oil

1/2 cup diced sweet onion

2 pounds heirloom tomatoes
(purply-red fleshed), quartered
and seeded

2 cups vegetable broth

1/4 cup chopped basil leaves

Salt and pepper

In an enamel-bottomed stockpot, heat the oil over medium heat. Add the onions and sauté for 5 minutes. Stir in the tomatoes and vegetable broth. Bring to a boil, then lower the heat and simmer for 20 minutes. Stir in the basil and continue simmering for 5 minutes. Blend with an immersion blender or puree in batches in a blender. Season to taste with salt and pepper. Keep warm over low heat.

## Spicy Tomato Soup

2 tablespoons olive oil

1/2 cup diced sweet onion

1 carrot, diced

1 celery stalk, diced

1/8 teaspoon cayenne pepper

2 pounds heirloom tomatoes
(yellow-orange fleshed),
quartered and seeded

2 cups water

Salt and pepper

In an enamel-bottomed stockpot, heat the oil over medium heat. Add the onions, carrots, celery, and cayenne pepper. Sauté, stirring occasionally, for 10 minutes. Add the tomatoes and water. Bring to a boil, then lower the heat and simmer for 20 minutes. Blend with an immersion blender or puree in batches in a blender. Season to taste with salt and pepper. Keep warm over low heat.

To serve, put each soup in an individual pitcher. Then simultaneously pour the soups from opposite sides into a serving bowl so that each half of the bowl is filled with a different soup. For an added touch, drag a knife or skewer through the darker soup into the lighter soup, creating an interesting design.

## SWEET CORN AND CHERRY TOMATO SALAD

Serves 4 to 6

6 ears of sweet corn (white and/or yellow), shucked

1 pint cherry tomatoes, cut in half

1 small sweet onion, cut in small dice (about 1/2 cup)

3 tablespoons red wine vinegar

3 tablespoons extra-virgin olive oil

Kosher salt and freshly ground pepper

1/2 cup thinly sliced fresh basil leaves

1/2 cup grated aged Gouda or Parmesan cheese

In a large pot of boiling water, cook the corn for 3 minutes, or just until the starchiness is gone. Drain. When the corn is cool, cut off the kernels, slicing close to the cob.

Toss the corn kernels in a large bowl with the tomatoes, onion, vinegar, olive oil, and salt and pepper to taste.

Just before serving, toss in the basil and cheese. Taste for seasoning and serve cold or at room temperature.

# LOBSTER MUSHROOMS WITH FENNEL AND TOMATO

Chef Seth Caswell, (formerly) Stumbling Goat Bistro, Seattle

Serves 8 (as a side dish)

1 pound lobster mushrooms

1 1/2 tablespoons extra-virgin olive oil, divided, plus more for garnish

Kosher salt and freshly ground pepper

1/2 cup dry white wine

2 fennel bulbs

2 pints mixed cherry tomatoes

2 teaspoons chopped fresh thyme

1 teaspoon thinly sliced fresh Berggarten sage

Brush off any dirt from the mushrooms with a coarse brush. Cut the mushrooms (if large) into quarters. Slice each mushroom piece into 1/4-inch-thick slices and set aside in a bowl.

Heat a large nonstick pan over high heat. Add 1 tablespoon olive oil and the mushrooms in a single layer. Sauté for three minutes and season to taste with salt and pepper. Add the wine to the pan and cook, stirring, to deglaze. Set aside.

Remove most of the fronds from the fennel bulbs. Thinly slice the fennel into long strips. Remove the stems from the tomatoes.

Heat a large sauté pan over medium heat. Add the tomatoes and cook until they begin to blister. Remove the tomatoes and add 1/2 tablespoon olive oil to the pan. Add the fennel and cook for 4 minutes, or until it begins to soften. Add the thyme, sage, salt and pepper to taste, and the blistered tomatoes.

Rewarm the mushrooms and toss with the fennel and tomato mixture. Transfer to a serving platter and garnish with a drizzle of olive oil.

## PARSNIP, TURNIP, AND CELERIAC PATTIES WITH TOMATILLO SALSA

Serves 6

Nonstick cooking spray

3 cups peeled and grated parsnips (about 3 large parsnips)

2 cups peeled and grated turnips (about 2 medium turnips)

1 cup peeled and grated celeriac

1 teaspoon salt

1/2 teaspoon celery seed

3 tablespoons butter, melted

1 cup Tomatillo Salsa (see below)

Preheat the oven to 425°F. Coat a baking sheet with cooking spray.

Place the grated root vegetables in a bowl. Mix in the salt and celery seed. Stir in the butter.

Mold the vegetable mixture into 6 patties by pressing into a 1/2-cup container and turning out onto the baking sheet. Press to flatten slightly. Bake for 15 minutes. Reduce the heat to 350°F, carefully flip the patties, and bake for 40 to 45 minutes, or until golden brown.

Serve with the salsa.

---

**Tomatillo Salsa**

1 pound tomatillos (about 5 medium), husked and rinsed

1/2 pound Anaheim peppers (about 2), rinsed

1/4 pound jalapeño peppers (about 2), rinsed

Preheat the broiler. Line a broiler pan with aluminum foil.

Place the tomatillos, whole, on the pan and broil for 7 minutes, or until a bit blackened. Turn over and broil the other side for 7 minutes. Remove the tomatillos from the pan and place on a rack to cool. Repeat the broiling process with the peppers.

Cut off the stem ends of the peppers, butterfly open, and remove the seeds. Cut off the stem ends of the tomatillos. Place all in a blender and puree for a second, just until blended.

Store in an airtight jar in the refrigerator until ready to use, up to 2 days.

## STONEY PLAINS ORGANIC FARM

Owners: Patricia Meyer and Patrick Meyer

Stoney Plains, a 60-acre farm producing 150 varieties of up to 50 crops, including beans, carrots, berries, and garlic, is the realization of Robert and Patricia Meyer's dream to make a wide variety of organic produce available to local communities. Through hard work, determination, and strong commitment, Patricia and her son Patrick, along with other family members — including grandkids — proudly continue to make Dad's dream come true.

## TAYLOR SHELLFISH FARMS

Owners: The Taylor Family

For over 100 years, the Taylor family has been growing shellfish in the inlets and bays of Puget Sound, situated in some of the most beautiful and pristine tidelands in the world. The Sound's clean, clear waters provide a perfect environment for harvesting flavorful and abundant shellfish. Taylor Shellfish has combined years of experience and modern technology to establish state-of-the-art farms that produce the finest-quality oysters, clams, mussels, and geoducks.

## MUSSELS PROVENÇAL

Chef John Howie, Seastar Restaurant and Raw Bar, Bellevue

Serves 6

3 tablespoons extra-virgin olive oil

3 garlic cloves, peeled and thinly sliced

1/4 cup minced white onion

3-4 pounds mussels, debearded

1 cup heirloom tomatoes cut in 1/2-inch dice

1 teaspoon sea salt

1 teaspoon freshly ground black pepper

2 ounces clam juice

2 ounces dry white wine

3 tablespoons coarsely chopped Italian parsley

Heat the olive oil in a large sauté pan over medium-high heat. Add the garlic and onion. Sauté until the garlic is turning golden.

Add the mussels to the pan and toss lightly. Add the tomatoes, salt, and pepper. Cook, tossing occasionally to ensure that the mussels are cooking evenly, about 2 minutes.

Add the clam juice and wine, lower the heat, and cover to steam for 2 minutes, or until the mussels have opened. Add the parsley and toss lightly. Place in a serving bowl and spoon some of the tomatoes over the top. Serve immediately.

## COCOA NIB CRUSTED LAMB LOINS

Chef Thomas Kollasch and Sous-Chef Adam Reece, Juno, Seattle

Serves 4

4  8-ounce boneless lamb loins

4 small shallots, diced

4 garlic cloves, sliced

4 teaspoons coarsely chopped fresh thyme

8 teaspoons sherry vinegar

3/4 cup grape seed oil

Salt and pepper

Pickled Cherry Mustard (see below)

Fennel and Cabbage Kraut (see below)

Cocoa Nib Mix (see below)

Demi-Glace (see below)

Combine the lamb, shallots, garlic, thyme, vinegar, and oil. Mix well and marinate for 6 to 8 hours or overnight.

Season the marinated lamb with salt and pepper to taste. In a large sauté pan, sear the lamb on both sides over medium-high heat to desired doneness.

Spread the cherry mustard equally onto 4 plates. Place equal portions of the kraut beside the mustard. Roll the lamb loins in the cocoa nib mix, then slice the coated lamb and fan the slices out on top of the kraut. Drizzle with a little demi-glace and serve immediately.

### Pickled Cherry Mustard

2 cups red wine vinegar

1/2 cup sugar

2 whole cloves

1 cinnamon stick

1 bay leaf

8 ounces sweet red cherries, pitted

1/2 cup Dijon mustard

Combine the vinegar, sugar, cloves, cinnamon, and bay leaf in a saucepan and bring to a boil. Reduce to a simmer and cook for 5 minutes. Pour into a plastic container with the cherries. Let the cherries soak overnight in the refrigerator. Strain the cherries, place in a blender, and puree. Add the mustard and blend until very smooth.

## Fennel and Cabbage Kraut

1/2 head green cabbage

2 fennel bulbs

1 tablespoon celery seed

4 juniper berries

1 bay leaf

1 cup sugar

1 teaspoon salt

Olive oil

1/2 cup diced yellow onion

1 tablespoon chopped fresh thyme

3 cups Riesling

Slice the cabbage and blanch in boiling water for 1 minute. Remove from the pot and immediately rinse under cold water to stop the cooking. Drain.

Thinly slice the fennel and mix it together with the cabbage.

Grind the celery seed, juniper berries, and bay leaf. Mix with the sugar and salt.

In a large heavy-duty bowl, combine the fennel/cabbage mixture with the sugar/salt mixture. Smash and knead the mixture with your hands to extract water from the fennel and cabbage. Cover the bowl and let the mixture marinate at room temperature overnight.

Rinse off the fennel and cabbage very well. Heat a nonreactive pan with olive oil to coat over medium heat. Add the onions and thyme and cook until the onions are translucent. Add the rinsed fennel and cabbage, cover, and braise for about 15 minutes. Add the Riesling, turn up the heat to medium-high, and cook until the wine has completely reduced.

## Cocoa Nib Mix

1/4 cup cocoa nibs*

2 teaspoons coriander seeds

Grind the ingredients together.

*Cocoa nibs are cocoa beans that have been roasted, separated from their husks, and ground into nibs. They are available at specialty chocolate stores (Theo Chocolate in Seattle).

## Demi-Glace

2 celery stalks

1 yellow onion

2 carrots

8 cups beef stock (low sodium)

1 fresh thyme sprig

1 bay leaf

4 black peppercorns

2 cups dry red wine

1 tablespoon cornstarch

Preheat the oven to 425°F.

Chop the celery, onion, and carrots into large pieces. Roast in the oven until they are a nice dark color.

Place the roasted vegetables in a large stockpot. Add the beef stock, thyme, bay leaf, and peppercorns. Bring to a boil, then lower the heat and simmer until reduced by half. Strain the stock and discard the vegetables. Return the stock to the pan.

Blend the wine and cornstarch. Stir into the stock and simmer until you have a nice rich flavor and the demi-glace coats the back of a spoon. This will take several hours.

# GINGER POT ROAST WITH VEGETABLES AND STAR ANISE

Chef Warren Seta, Yama at the Galleria, Bellevue

Serves 6 to 8

2 tablespoons olive oil

3-4 pounds beef chuck, or any other type of braising beef

Salt and pepper

1 medium-sized onion, cut into large quarters

4 garlic cloves, peeled and whole

2 ounces fresh ginger, peeled and cut into 1/8-inch-thick medallions

1 teaspoon crushed red pepper

8-10 fresh shiitake mushrooms, stemmed and halved

1/2 to 3/4 bottle dry red wine

2 tablespoons soy sauce (low sodium)

1 cup beef stock

1 tablespoon toasted sesame oil

2 tablespoons sugar

2 whole star anise

1/2 pound baby carrots, peeled and whole

1 pound fingerling or red potatoes, unpeeled and whole if small, halved otherwise

Crusty French bread or steamed white rice, for serving

Heat a Dutch oven or heavy pot over medium-high heat with olive oil. Rinse the meat under cold water, pat dry, and season liberally with salt and pepper. Sear the meat on all sides until well caramelized, about 2 minutes per side. Remove the meat and set aside.

Add the onions, garlic, ginger, red pepper, and mushrooms to the pot and sauté for about 3 minutes. Add the wine, soy sauce, beef stock, sesame oil, sugar, and star anise. Stir until the sugar is dissolved and well incorporated.

Return the meat to the pot. The liquid should come to just below the top edge of the beef once you have nestled it down into the pot. If not, add more beef stock or water. Reduce the heat to low, cover the pot, and allow to slow-cook for 4 to 5 hours. This should be a slow simmer and not a boil. Check every hour. If too much evaporation of the liquid takes place, add more water or beef stock.

About 30 minutes before the beef is done, place the carrots and potatoes on top of the roast, cover, and resume cooking. The beef is done when it falls apart and the sauce is slightly thickened.

Remove the star anise before serving. Enjoy with crusty French bread for dipping or even atop some steamed white rice.

## SUGAR PIE PUMPKIN PIE

Pastry Chef Sandra Watson, Trellis, Kirkland

Serves 8

**Crust**

1 1/4 cups all-purpose flour, plus more for dusting

1/2 teaspoon salt

1/2 cup unsalted butter, cold, cut into small pieces

2 tablespoons cold water, more if needed

**Pie**

2-3 pounds Sugar Pie pumpkin (2 cups of cooked puree)

Nonstick cooking spray

1/2 teaspoon pumpkin pie spice

1/2 teaspoon kosher salt

1/2 teaspoon vanilla extract

2 large whole eggs

2 large egg yolks

1/3 cup firmly packed light brown sugar

2 cups heavy cream

To make the crust, whisk together the flour and salt in a large bowl. Cut in the butter pieces with a pastry blender or by hand until the dough looks like coarse crumbs with some pea-sized pieces. Add the water in small quantities, stirring into the flour mixture until the dough holds together. To test if it is done, squeeze a small amount together. If it sticks together, it is done; if it is crumbly, add more water, a tablespoon at a time.

Press the dough into a flat disk and wrap in plastic. Refrigerate for at least 30 minutes or overnight.

On a lightly floured surface, roll out the dough larger than a 9-inch pie pan. Brush off excess flour and carefully fold the dough in half. Lift into the pie pan, with the fold in the center. Open out the dough, fitting into the pan and pressing into the edges. Cut off overhanging dough, leaving about 1/2 inch all around. Crimp the edges as desired. Freeze the crust for 1 hour.

Preheat the oven to 375°F. Since the crust is frozen, you do not need to weight down the crust while baking. Fit a buttered piece of aluminum foil into the pie shell, buttered side down. Place on a baking sheet and bake in the center of the oven for 25 minutes. Carefully remove the foil. If the crust has puffed while baking, gently press it down with the back of a spoon. Return to the oven and bake, watching carefully, until lightly golden. Transfer to a rack to cool completely.

Preheat the oven to 400°F. Halve the pumpkin, remove seeds and strings, and place cut-side down on a baking pan coated with cooking spray. Roast until very soft, about 1 hour. Scrape out the flesh and puree. Place the puree in a fine-mesh strainer over a bowl and let drain for 2 hours. Discard the liquid.

Preheat the oven to 325°F. Whisk together the pumpkin puree, pumpkin pie spice, salt, and vanilla. Whisk in the whole eggs and egg yolks until thoroughly blended. Add the sugar and heavy cream and mix until combined.

Pour the mixture into the prebaked pie shell and bake for 35 to 40 minutes, or until the custard is set but still has some jiggle in the center. Transfer to a rack to cool.

# SNAPPY APPLE TART

Serves 8

## Applesauce

6 medium cooking apples –
Rome or other red-skinned
cooking apples are best

1 tablespoon packed light
brown sugar

1/4 cup water

## Crust

1 1/4 cups all-purpose flour

1/2 cup confectioners' sugar

1/4 cup sifted gingersnap
cookie crumbs (or try Tall Grass
Bakery's molasses cookie)

1/4 teaspoon salt

9 tablespoons cold
unsalted butter, cut into
very small pieces

1 large egg yolk, slightly beaten

To prepare the applesauce, core the apples and cut into chunks, with the skin left on. Mix the brown sugar and water in a large enamel-bottomed pot. Stir in the apples, cover the pot, and set over medium heat. Keep watching the pot and stir often so the apples don't scorch. When the apples are soft enough to mash — about 15 minutes — remove from the heat and either put through a food mill or mash by hand until you have a smooth and beautifully pink applesauce. If you are mashing by hand, be sure to remove the skins. If liquid accumulates around the rim of the bowl, return the applesauce to the pot and heat, stirring, for a few minutes to thicken. Put the applesauce back in the bowl. Press a piece of plastic wrap against the surface, tightly cover, and refrigerate until completely cooled. This can be made a few days ahead and stored in the refrigerator.

To make the crust, sift together the flour, sugar, cookie crumbs, and salt into a large bowl. Add the butter pieces and quickly cut into the flour mixture with a pastry cutter or your fingers until you have a crumbly mixture. Make a well in the middle and add the slightly beaten egg yolk. Mix together with your fingers until the dough forms a ball.

Place the dough in the center of a buttered 9-inch tart pan and press evenly over the bottom and up the sides. If the dough goes over the edges of the pan, press a rolling pin across the top to remove the excess. Freeze the crust for 1 hour.

Preheat the oven to 375°F. Since the crust is frozen, you do not need pie weights for baking. Butter the shiny side of a piece of aluminum foil and place it, buttered side down, on the dough, pressing to fit tightly. Set the tart pan on a baking sheet, place on the center oven rack, and bake for 25 minutes. Carefully remove the foil. If the crust has puffed while baking, use the back of a spoon to gently press the dough back down. If the bottom is not cooked as much as the sides, return the crust to the oven for a few minutes, checking continually to prevent overbrowning. Remove from the oven and let cool on a rack to room temperature.

### Topping

2 tablespoons sugar, divided

1/2 teaspoon ground cinnamon

1/4 teaspoon ground ginger

1 tablespoon butter

2 medium apples, peeled, cored, and cut into 1/2-inch slices – Granny Smiths work well

Juice of 1/2 lemon

To prepare the topping, mix together 1 tablespoon sugar, cinnamon, and ginger in a small bowl and set aside. Melt the butter in a large saucepan over low heat. Coat the apple slices with the remaining tablespoon of sugar. Place in the saucepan in a single layer and sauté for 2 minutes per side. Sprinkle with the cinnamon sugar mixture and turn to carefully coat the slices. Drizzle with lemon juice and continue stirring for 2 minutes. Remove from the heat and let cool.

Preheat the oven to 400°F.

To assemble the tart, fill the tart shell with applesauce to just below the rim of the crust. Place the apple slices on top, slightly overlapping, in 2 concentric circles.

Place the tart on a baking sheet. Set on the center oven rack and bake for 45 minutes, or until the crust is golden brown. Let the tart cool on a rack until just warm or room temperature.

## MARTIN FAMILY ORCHARDS

Owners: Rick and Terri Martin

Set on a stunning hillside with a breathtaking view of the Columbia River, Rick and Terri's home sits among the orchards in Orondo, about 30 minutes outside Wenatchee. For over 20 years, this family farm, run by Rick, Terri, and their three sons, has been a presence at markets on both sides of the Cascades. All of the fruit on their 80 acres is picked tree-ripe for the most flavorful eating. The farm also cooperates with nature by having ladybugs and lacewings integrated into their pest management.

# MARKET
# STAPLES

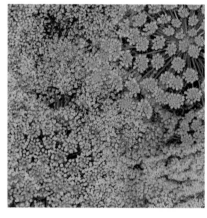

**PANTRY TIPS**

**FROM THE SOURCE: PRESTON HILL BAKERY**

**RECIPES:**

ROASTED PEPPER SOUP

ITALIAN BEAN SOUP

PANZANELLA (BREAD SALAD)

GREENS WITH GOAT CHEESE AND WARM MUSHROOMS

SAVOY CABBAGE AND BABY CARROT SALAD

PENNE WITH FRESH AND ROASTED TOMATO SAUCE

VERACI THIN-CRUST PIZZA

HOMEMADE VERACI PESTO

SHEPHERD'S PIE

ARUGULA PESTO ATOP LA PASTA'S PUMPKIN RAVIOLI

PAVLOVA WITH BERRIES

HAZELNUT SHORTBREAD COOKIES

# PANTRY TIPS

**Albacore Tuna**
Canned, jerky, and smoked versions will last a long time. Keep in a cool, dry place.

**Breads**
Bread bought at the market will not last as long as store-bought bread with added preservatives. To keep market breads longer, slice and place in resealable plastic freezer bags and store in the freezer. Take out a slice and toast/defrost in the toaster whenever you like!

**Cider**
Keep in the refrigerator or a cool place. Bring back your empty jugs to recycle.

**Dried Beans**
Store at room temperature in an airtight container. Do not refrigerate.

To soak dried beans: Place beans in a large pot with enough water to totally submerge them. Cover and refrigerate, soaking for 6 to 8 hours or overnight. Drain and rinse. Lentils, split peas, and black-eyed peas do not need to be soaked.

To cook dried beans: In a large stockpot, add beans and three times as much water, covering the beans by about 1 inch. Bring to a boil, reduce the heat, cover, and simmer for about 1 hour, or until the beans are tender. Check occasionally and add water if the beans aren't submerged. Beans are done when they can be easily mashed with a fork . . . or your fingers. Drain. They are now ready to be used in a recipe.

**Dried Fruit**
Kept in an airtight container, dried fruit will last in your pantry for about six months.

**Dried Mushrooms**
Store in an airtight container. To use, place the mushrooms in a bowl and cover with boiling water. Seal the bowl with plastic wrap to keep in the steam for 5 to 10 minutes, or until the mushrooms are tender. Drain. They are now ready to be used in a recipe.

**Frozen Meats**
Frozen meats will keep in an airtight container in the freezer for about one year.

To thaw: The best way is to place frozen meat on a tray on the bottom shelf of the refrigerator in the original wrapping until completely defrosted. It usually takes about five hours per pound for thicker cuts of meat, less time for thinner cuts. You can also use a cold-water bath to defrost by placing packaged frozen meat in a container of cold water. Change the water every 30 minutes and reposition the meat to thaw evenly.

**Frozen Salmon**
This will keep in its airtight packaging for a few months.

To thaw: Place frozen fish in its original wrappings in a tray on the bottom shelf of the refrigerator until completely thawed. The slow thawing helps keep in the juices; it will take about eight hours per pound to defrost.

## Hazelnut Oil

Oils are sensitive to light and exposure to oxygen, so it's best to keep this in the refrigerator or a cool, dry place. It should last for about three months.

## Hazelnuts

Hazelnuts will keep in an airtight container in the refrigerator for one year. They can also be stored in a cool, dry place, but will not keep as long.

## Honey

Store honey in an airtight container in a cool, dry place. It will keep for a very long time! If you keep it in the refrigerator, honey will thicken. If it is stored in too warm an environment, its flavor may change and its color may darken. If the honey crystallizes, put the container in hot water for about 15 minutes to get it back to a liquid. Return your empty jars for recycling.

## Jams

Stock your pantry with some of the market's jams, or try making your own with all of the incredibly fresh fruit throughout the market's seasons. Ask the farmer about recycling the empty jars.

## Pasta

Place the frozen container of pasta in a resealable plastic freezer bag and store in the freezer for a few months. Keep frozen until ready to use.

## Roasted Peppers

You will often see farmers roasting peppers at the market in the fall. Put the roasted peppers in resealable plastic freezer bags and store in the freezer. They're a great addition to soups or lasagna.

For a quick treat, go through the market collecting your favorite bread, cheese, roasted peppers, fresh greens of your choice, and perhaps a little chimichurri or hummus. Slice the bread, spread with chimichurri or hummus, add cheese, peppers, and greens. You can even dine on this delicious sandwich while shopping at the market!

To roast at home: Toss peppers with a little olive oil and either roast in a 400°F oven for about 1 hour, until tender, or broil on the highest oven rack until the skins are blistered and blackened. To remove the skins more easily, place the roasted peppers in a large bowl and cover with plastic wrap. The steam will loosen the skins. Once cool to the touch, peel off the skin and use the peppers in a recipe or store in resealable plastic freezer bags for later use.

## Vinegar

Store tightly closed in a cool, dark place. Vinegar will last for about a year after it is opened.

## Wine

The fruit wines at the market all have a different taste and can be served at different temperatures. Ask the farmer about the best way to serve and what each is best paired with . . . and, of course, bring back the empties!

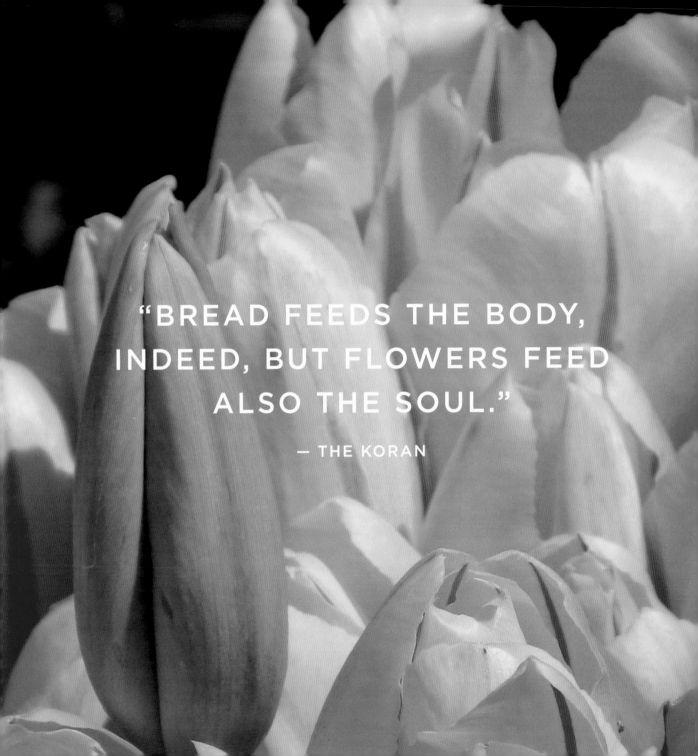

"BREAD FEEDS THE BODY,
INDEED, BUT FLOWERS FEED
ALSO THE SOUL."

— THE KORAN

## PRESTON HILL BAKERY

Owner: Alex Williams

After 20 years as an architect/builder, Alex took advantage of a new direction and followed his passion for baking. He apprenticed as a baker for five years, with stops at Grand Central Bakery, La Panzanella Bakery, and Palace Kitchen Restaurant. In 2006, after a pilgrimage to several California artisan bakeries, he decided to utilize his background to build a wholesale bakery and wood-fired oven on his property in Preston. Toast a slice of Preston Hill Bakery's chocolate bun bread. Spread with peanut butter. Tastes like a Reese's!

"My passion for handmade artisan bread has led me to build my own bakery and wood-fired brick oven. I use organic ingredients and hand mix, form, and bake this European-style bread to recapture the primitive quality of a simple, delicious loaf." — Alex Williams

# RECILES

## ROASTED PEPPER SOUP

Serves 6

6 bell peppers (any color except green)

3 tablespoons olive oil, plus more to brush peppers

1 cup diced carrots

1/2 cup diced sweet onion

1/2 cup diced fennel bulb

6 cups chicken broth

1 tablespoon herbes de Provence

1/4 teaspoon crushed red pepper

Salt and pepper

Your choice of market-fresh goat cheese

Preheat the broiler.

Cut the peppers into quarters, core, and seed. Place skin-side up on a broiler pan. Brush lightly with olive oil. Broil until the skins are blistered and blackened. Let the peppers cool, then rub off the skin and slice into strips.

Heat 3 tablespoons olive oil in a stockpot over medium heat. Add the roasted peppers, carrots, onions, and fennel. Cook, stirring occasionally, for 10 to 15 minutes.

Add the chicken broth and bring to a boil. Reduce the heat. Add the herbes de Provence and crushed red pepper. Simmer, partially covered, for about 30 minutes.

Puree in small batches in a blender. Reheat. Add salt and pepper to taste.

To serve, place a small slice of cheese on the bottom of each bowl. Pour hot soup over the top. Stir before eating or leave as a pleasant surprise with each bite!

## BILLY'S GARDEN

Owners: Billy and Stephanie Allstot

Billy and Stephanie Allstot grow certified organic fruits and vegetables on their family farm in Tonasket, roughly a five-hour drive from Bellevue. Billy's Garden supplies many farmers' markets and popular restaurants with their bounty. Besides numerous varieties of peaches and heirloom tomatoes, Billy's produces not only the familiar red and green peppers, but also the more exotic chocolate, ivory, and lilac varieties. A specialty of theirs is roasting fresh peppers on-site at markets, ready for you to enjoy in a favorite dish at home or in a sandwich created right at the market.

## ITALIAN BEAN SOUP

Serves 6

1 pound dried cannellini beans

2 tablespoons olive oil

1 cup diced carrots

1/2 cup diced celery

1/2 cup diced onion

2 tablespoons tomato paste

2 cups chopped Savoy cabbage

3 cups chopped dark kale
(cavolo nero)

4 cups chicken broth

6 fresh thyme sprigs

Salt and pepper

Parmigiano-Reggiano
cheese, grated (optional)

Soak the beans overnight in water, covered, in the refrigerator. Drain and rinse. Place the beans in a large pot with enough water to cover by 1 to 2 inches. Bring to a boil, reduce the heat, and simmer for at least 1 hour, or until tender. Drain and rinse.

Heat the olive oil in a large stockpot over medium heat. Add the carrots, celery, and onion. Cook until the onion is translucent, about 10 minutes. Add the tomato paste, stirring to combine well with the vegetables. Stir in the cabbage and kale and cook for 5 minutes before adding the broth, beans, and thyme. Cover and simmer for 2 hours. Remove the thyme sprigs.

To thicken the soup, puree 2 cups of the soup. Return to the pot and season to taste with salt and pepper.

Sprinkle individual bowls of soup with grated cheese, if desired.

For a heartier soup, add sautéd sliced Italian sausage about 1 hour before serving.

## PANZANELLA (BREAD SALAD)

Executive Chef Brian Gojdics and Chef Anthony Ferrara, Tutta Bella Neapolitan Pizzeria, Seattle

Serves 8 to 10

1 loaf day-old rustic bread, sliced

3 or more tablespoons extra-virgin olive oil

3 ripe tomatoes, sliced and seeded

1 small sweet red onion, sliced

1/4 cup chopped fresh basil

2 tablespoons minced fresh parsley (optional)

1 garlic clove, minced (optional)

1 teaspoon balsamic vinegar (more to taste)

Salt and freshly ground pepper

Prepare a charcoal or gas grill.

Brush the bread slices with olive oil and grill each side for about 2 minutes. Set aside to cool.

Mix the tomatoes, onions, herbs, garlic, and vinegar in a large bowl.

Cut the grilled bread into 3/4-inch pieces and toss with the other ingredients. Season to taste with salt and pepper and serve immediately.

Feel free to add fresh mozzarella, cucumbers, olives, canned tuna, or whatever else you have. This is a versatile dish.

## GREENS WITH GOAT CHEESE AND WARM MUSHROOMS

Willie Green's Organic Farm, Monroe

Serves 4

8 ounces Willie Green's mixed baby greens

2 ounces soft, fresh goat cheese, crumbled

6 tablespoons olive oil

8 ounces mixed fresh wild mushrooms, trimmed and thinly sliced

4 teaspoons chopped mixed fresh herbs (such as basil, thyme, and rosemary)

Salt and pepper

1/4 cup red wine vinegar

1 teaspoon chopped fresh chives

Divide the greens among 4 plates. Sprinkle with goat cheese.

Heat the oil in a large heavy skillet over medium-high heat. Add the mushrooms and mixed herbs. Sauté until the mushrooms are tender, about 3 minutes. Season to taste with salt and pepper.

Remove from the heat and stir in the vinegar. Divide the mushrooms and liquid equally over the greens. Sprinkle with chives and serve immediately.

## WILLIE GREEN'S ORGANIC FARM

Owner: Jeff Miller

Willie Green's Organic Farm is a small family farm in Monroe owned and operated by Jeff Miller, a classically trained chef-turned-farmer. From a humble quarter acre in 1985 to today's 27 acres, Willie Green's has built a reputation for growing the very finest organic greens and produce. Never content to rest on that reputation, they strive to maintain the strictest quality standards. Willie Green's continues testing new varieties to provide the most flavorful produce. Superior varieties are grown in volume and brought to the markets.

## SAVOY CABBAGE AND BABY CARROT SALAD

Chef Seth Caswell, (formerly) Stumbling Goat Bistro, Seattle

Serves 8

1 bunch salad burnet

1 bunch bronze fennel

1 bunch chives

1 bunch mint

1 bunch lovage

1 bunch tarragon

1 bunch sweet cicely

2 tablespoons extra-virgin olive oil, divided, plus more for brushing peppers

1 teaspoon red wine vinegar

Kosher salt and freshly ground pepper to taste

1 pound mixed sweet peppers

1 bunch white pearl onions

1 bunch Thumbelina carrots

2 Savoy cabbages

Wash and dry all the herbs (burnet, fennel, chives, mint, lovage, tarragon, and sweet cicely) and pick the leaves off each of the bunches. The chives can be cut into 1/2-inch lengths, and the tarragon can be lightly chopped if the leaves are large. Mix the herbs together and set aside, covered lightly with a damp towel.

In a medium bowl, whisk together 1 tablespoon of the olive oil, vinegar, salt, and pepper. Just before serving, add the herb mixture and toss with salt and pepper.

Preheat the broiler to high. Cut the peppers into quarters, core, and seed. Place skin-side up on a broiler pan. Brush lightly with olive oil. Broil until the skins are blistered and blackened. Let the peppers cool, then rub off the skin and roughly chop.

Peel and cut the onions in half. Cut the carrots into very thin slices (use a mandoline if you have one). Shred the cabbage with a knife.

Heat the remaining tablespoon of olive oil in a large sauté pan over high heat. Add the onions and carrots and sauté for 3 minutes, until the edges of the carrots begin to brown. Add the cabbage, cover, and cook for an additional 6 minutes. Remove the cover, season with salt and pepper, and let the liquid in the pan evaporate for 1 minute. Stir in the roasted peppers.

Place the vegetables on 8 salad plates. Top with the herb mixture. Serve hot or at room temperature.

## PENNE WITH FRESH AND ROASTED TOMATO SAUCE

Chef Jacky Lo, Bennett's Pure Food Bistro, Mercer Island

Serves 4

### Pasta

2 tablespoons olive oil

3 ounces zucchini, diced

2 ounces sweet onion, chopped fine

2 ounces mushrooms, quartered

Salt and pepper

3 ounces fresh tomato, diced

1 small tomato, roasted and chopped (see note)

4 cherry tomatoes, halved

4 ounces Fresh Tomato Sauce (see below)

1 pound penne pasta, cooked al dente and drained

1 teaspoon chopped fresh parsley, divided

1/2 ounce Fontina cheese, shredded

### Fresh Tomato Sauce

1/4 cup olive oil

4 garlic cloves, chopped

6 tomatoes, chopped

1 tablespoon salt

1/3 cup chopped fresh basil

Heat the olive oil in a medium-sized sauté pan over high heat. Add the zucchini, onion, and mushrooms and sauté until browned. Season to taste with salt and pepper.

Add the tomatoes and sauté for another minute or two, then stir in the tomato sauce.

Add the cooked pasta and toss well. Season to taste with salt and pepper. Add half of the parsley and toss until the pasta is hot. Garnish each serving with the remaining parsley and Fontina.

Note: To roast tomatoes, preheat the oven to 350°F. Cut the tomatoes in half, toss with olive oil to coat, and season with salt and pepper. Place cut-side up on a baking sheet and roast until the skins are wrinkled.

In a medium stainless steel pan, heat the olive oil over medium-low heat. Add the garlic and sauté for about 1 minute. Add the tomatoes, turn the heat up to medium-high, and cook until the tomatoes are falling apart, about 20 minutes.

Puree the sauce with an immersion blender (or in a food processor). Stir in the salt and basil. Taste and adjust salt if needed. Refrigerate for up to 7 days or freeze. Makes 2 quarts.

## VERACI THIN-CRUST PIZZA

Chef Marshall Jett, Veraci Pizza, Seattle

Makes four 14-inch pizzas

2 cups warm water (100°F)

1/2 teaspoon active dry yeast

1 teaspoon turbinado natural cane sugar

6 cups all-purpose unbleached flour (unsifted)

1 teaspoon sea salt

2 tablespoons extra-virgin olive oil

Your favorite toppings (including the Homemade Veraci Pesto recipe that follows)

Special equipment: pizza stone

Pour the warm water into a large mixing bowl. Add the yeast and sugar and mix together with a whisk. As you continue to mix, add 3 cups of flour. Mix thoroughly. The dough should be very thick and lump-free. Remove the whisk and set aside.

Place 2 cups of flour in a pile in the middle of the counter or a large cutting board. With your hand, form an 8-inch circular depression in the middle of the flour, leaving a small amount of flour on the bottom. Using a rubber spatula, transfer the dough into the middle of the flour. Slowly fold small amounts of flour from the edges into the middle, blending it thoroughly as you go. Avoid adding the flour too quickly, which results in dry spots or lumps. Scrape the counter and add more flour underneath if necessary to prevent sticking. Sprinkle small amounts of the flour onto the top of the dough as you fold. Continue until the dough is workable by hand — not too loose or sticky. Mix in the sea salt.

Knead the dough for about 3 minutes. Cut the dough in half and look at the interior; if the dough is too soft, it will quickly slump down. In this case, continue kneading and add more flour. The dough is ready when the interior remains upright or slumps very slightly when cut. If too much flour is added, the dough will be unworkable.

Cut the dough into 4 pieces. Shape each into a ball, coat with olive oil, and set aside to proof for at least 30 minutes. Place the pizza stone on the lower rack in the oven and preheat the oven to 450-550°F.

Using a rolling pin, roll out each ball of dough on a floured work surface. To make a round pizza, flip the dough over and over, turning it each time so that you roll it in many different directions. Add more flour to both sides as needed to avoid sticking, and fix any holes by pinching the dough back together.

When the dough is about 14 inches wide, lightly dust the top with flour. Flip the entire pizza over and onto a wooden peel. (If you do not have a peel, use a cookie sheet.) Decorate the pizza with a layer of sauce or olive oil, a light layer of cheese, and other delicious market toppings of your choice. Less is more.

Lightly pat down the toppings and test-shake the pizza to make sure it moves on the peel. Slide the pizza onto the hot pizza stone in the oven and cook for 5 to 7 minutes, or until the outer crust is golden brown. (If you are using a cookie sheet, transfer it directly to the hot oven.) Remove the pizza from the oven and let cool slightly before serving.

## HOMEMADE VERACI PESTO

Chef Marshall Jett, Veraci Pizza, Seattle

Yield: about 4 cups

1 large or 2 medium bunches fresh market basil

1 1/2-2 cups good-quality olive oil

1 1/2-2 cups imported Pecorino Romano cheese cut into 1/2-inch cubes*

3-4 medium-sized fresh garlic cloves, peeled

Wash the basil thoroughly in cold water. Dry it completely in a towel. Next, remove the majority of the stalks from the basil by twisting them off or chopping them. Discard any discolored leaves. Put the remaining basil leaves (a few stalks are OK) into a food processor. Secure the cover and start the machine. Pour in enough olive oil to liquefy the basil (about 1 cup).

Immediately add the Pecorino, a few cubes at a time, and the garlic. Be prepared for some serious shakin'! Slowly add enough of the remaining olive oil to thin the mixture. After all the ingredients have been added, blend for about a minute. The pesto is ready when the tiny bits of basil and Pecorino are the size of coarse sand. The consistency should be that of a thick, spreadable sauce.

Use your rubber spatula to transfer the pesto to a bowl. Place plastic wrap directly on top of the pesto to prevent discoloration if you are not going to use it immediately. It will last for about five days in the fridge. Do not freeze.

Serving suggestions: Homemade pesto is a delicious topping for pasta, pizza, or fresh seafood. Or you can spread it on slices of a Tall Grass Bakery baguette and serve as an appetizer.

*Imported Parmigiano-Reggiano can be used in place of the Pecorino Romano.

## SHEPHERD'S PIE

Skagit River Ranch, Sedro-Woolley

Serves 6 to 8

1 pound ground beef

3 strips bacon, diced

1 small onion, chopped

2 garlic cloves, minced

1/4 teaspoon dried oregano

1/2 cup tomato sauce

1 can (2.25 ounces) sliced ripe olives, drained and chopped

5 1/2 cups hot mashed potatoes (prepared without milk or butter)

2 eggs, beaten

2 tablespoons butter, softened

1 tablespoon minced fresh cilantro or parsley

1/4 teaspoon salt

Additional butter, melted

Preheat the oven to 375°F.

In a skillet, cook the ground beef over medium heat, stirring to crumble, until it is no longer pink; drain and set aside.

In the same skillet, cook the bacon, onion, garlic, and oregano until the bacon is crisp. Stir in the tomato sauce, olives, and beef. Simmer for 10 minutes.

Meanwhile, combine the mashed potatoes, eggs, butter, cilantro or parsley, and salt; mix well. Spread half of the potato mixture onto the bottom and up the sides of a greased 9-inch pie plate. Top with the beef mixture, then the remaining potato mixture.

Bake for 20 minutes. Brush with melted butter, then bake for 10 more minutes, or until golden brown.

## SKAGIT RIVER RANCH

Owners: George and Eiko Vojkovich

Skagit River Ranch is a small family-owned organic farm in the fertile Skagit Valley about 90 minutes north of Seattle. They have spent 15 years providing customers with the most wholesome, best-tasting organic 100% grass-fed beef, pork, pasture-raised chicken, and fresh eggs available. Skagit River's commitment is to farm in harmony with their environment.

Serves 4

2 cups arugula, stems removed

1/2 cup olive oil

1/4 teaspoon salt

1/3 cup chopped walnuts

1 package (1 pound) La Pasta's Pumpkin Ravioli (frozen)

Have a large bowl of iced water at the ready. Bring a medium pot of water to a boil. Add the arugula for 1 minute. Remove with a slotted spoon and immediately submerge in iced water to stop the cooking. Transfer the arugula to a towel to drain. Roll up the towel and carefully squeeze out excess water.

Place the arugula in a food processor. Add the olive oil, salt, and walnuts. Process until well blended.

Cook the frozen ravioli as directed on the package. Top with the pesto.

The pesto should be used immediately or stored in an airtight container in the refrigerator for up to 5 days.

# PAVLOVA WITH BERRIES

Serves 10 to 12

Parchment paper

4 large egg whites, at
room temperature

1 teaspoon vanilla extract

1/2 teaspoon cream of tartar

1 cup superfine sugar

## Topping

Berries (or fruit of choice),
fresh or frozen

1 pint heavy cream

2 tablespoons superfine sugar

Preheat the oven to 200°F. Grease and flour the sides of a
9-inch springform pan. Line the bottom with parchment paper,
cut to fit the pan.

In a large mixer on medium speed, whisk together the egg
whites, vanilla, and cream of tartar until soft peaks form.
Increase the speed to high and add the sugar a spoonful
at a time, beating until very stiff peaks form.

Spoon the meringue into the prepared pan, spreading out
evenly. Bake for 2 hours. Turn off the oven and leave the
meringue in the oven to cool completely. If you're not using
the meringue immediately, store it in an airtight container.
Do not refrigerate or freeze.

To prepare the topping, if the berries (or fruit) are frozen, thaw
completely and drain off the juices. Whisk the cream and sugar
together until stiff peaks form.

Spread the whipped cream on top of the cooled meringue,
leaving about 1 inch of meringue showing around the edges.
Top with the fruit.

## HAZELNUT SHORTBREAD COOKIES

Makes 6 dozen 2-inch round cookies

3 sticks unsalted butter, at room temperature

1 cup sugar

1 teaspoon vanilla extract

1 teaspoon lemon extract

3 1/2 cups flour

1/4 teaspoon salt

1 1/2 cups chopped hazelnuts*

Cream together the butter and sugar. Add the vanilla and lemon extracts.

In a separate bowl, sift together the flour and salt. Add to the butter mixture, stirring until blended. Stir in the chopped hazelnuts. Divide the dough into 2 flattened disks and wrap in plastic wrap. Chill in the refrigerator for 30 minutes.

Preheat the oven to 350°F.

Roll the dough out to 1/4 inch thick and cut into shapes with the cookie cutter of choice. Place on an ungreased baking sheet. Bake for 20 minutes, or until lightly golden. Transfer to a cooling rack.

*Option: Substitute 1/2 cup chopped dried cherries for the chopped hazelnuts.

## HOLMQUIST HAZELNUT ORCHARDS

Owner: The Holmquist Family

Just a short drive from Lynden and the Canadian border, Holmquist Hazelnut Orchards is nestled in the heart of Whatcom County and is one of the largest hazelnut-producing orchards in Washington. John Holmquist and his son, Anton, planted the first orchard in 1928, taking advantage of the Pacific Northwest's rich soil and mild weather. Five generations later, the Holmquist family continues to take pride in offering the finest-quality hazelnuts. Much of their success is due to the DuChilly hazelnut, a sweeter variety that does not have the bitter skin found on the common round hazelnut. Throughout the years, one thing has always remained the same — a quality and freshness of product that speaks for itself.

# Bellevue Farmers Market

spring has sprung... the new season has begun!!

Welcome to
our new vendors:

* billy's garden - tonasket
* mt. townsend creamery - port townsend
* wooly pigs - spokane
* pete's perfect butter toffee - mountlake terrace
* little prague bakery - seattle
* pan africa market - seattle

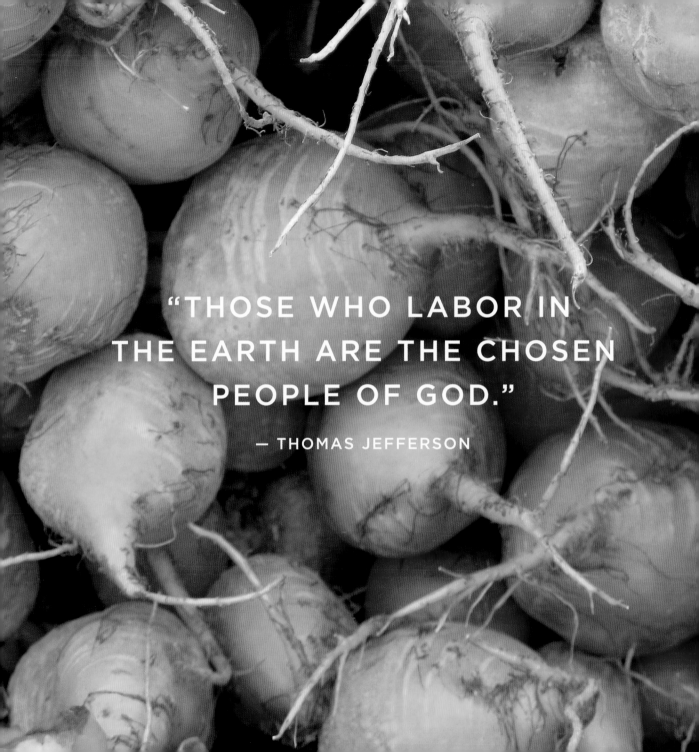

"THOSE WHO LABOR IN THE EARTH ARE THE CHOSEN PEOPLE OF GOD."

— THOMAS JEFFERSON

## MARKET VENDORS

Thank you to all of these farmers and vendors that participated in the Bellevue Farmers Market in the 2008 season. This list shows where the vendors travel from and what they bring to the market, and for most of the farms, it also shows their acreage.

### FARMS

**Alm Hill Gardens**
Everson; 30 acres
organic produce, berries, flowers

**Billy's Garden**
Tonasket; 49 acres
organic produce, plant starts,
berries, peaches

**Booth Canyon Orchard**
Carlton; 7.5 acres
organic apples, peaches, pears, plums

**Canales Produce**
Concrete/Yakima; 97.5 acres
organic produce, berries, grapes

**Crawford Blueberries**
Prosser; 80 acres
blueberries, sweet corn

**Delap Orchards**
Malott; 110 acres
apples, apricots, cherries, nectarines, peaches,
pears, plums, pluots

**Full Circle Farm**
Carnation; 260 acres
organic produce, berries

**Golden Glen Creamery**
Bow; 145 acres
butter, cheese, cream, milk

**Hayton Farms**
Mount Vernon; 150 acres
berries

**Heavenscent Lavender**
Clyde Hill; .5 acre
lavender

**Hedlin Family Farms**
Mount Vernon; 400 acres
organic produce, berries, flowers

**Holmquist Hazelnut Orchards**
Lynden; 80 acres
hazelnuts

**Homestead Organic Produce**
Quincy; 150 acres
organic produce, berries, melons

**Kittitas Valley Greenhouse**
Ellensburg; .25 acre
heirloom tomatoes, cucumbers, peppers

**Lee Lor Garden**
Carnation; 8 acres
flowers, herbs, vegetables

**Martin Family Orchards**
Orondo; 80 acres
apples, apricots, cherries, nectarines, peaches,
pears, pluots

**Pipitone Farms**
Rock Island; 5 acres
organic apricots, peaches, shallots,
Italian garlic, nectarines, tomatoes

**Port Madison Farm**
Bainbridge Island; 16 acres
goat cheese, yogurt

**Razey Orchards**
Naches; 21 acres
organic cherries

**River Farm**
Ellensburg; 21 acres
organic produce, chicken, melons,
peppers, plant starts

**Rockridge Orchards**
Enumclaw; 41 acres
cider, wine, produce, apples, Asian pears,
berries, grapes, plums, honey

**Schmidt Blueberry Farm**
Marysville; 4 acres
blueberries

**Shua's Vegetables and Flowers**
Carnation; 4 acres
flowers, vegetables

**Skagit River Ranch**
Sedro-Woolley; 200 acres
organic, grass-fed beef, chicken, pork, eggs

**Stoney Plains Organic Farm**
Tenino; 47 acres
organic produce, berries,
plant starts

**Sua Yang Farm**
Monroe; 15 acres
flowers, vegetables

**Tahuya River Apiaries**
Tahuya
honey

**Thai Yang & Chee Her Garden**
Monroe; 2 acres
flowers, vegetables

**Tiny's Organic**
Wenatchee; 67 acres
organic apples, apriums, cherries, nectarines,
peaches, plums, pluots

**Willie Green's Organic Farm**
Monroe; 52 acres
organic produce, berries

**Wooly Pigs**
Spokane; 100 acres
Berkshire and Mangalitsa pork

**Yang Garden**
Carnation; 5 acres
flowers, vegetables

**Youa Her & Kaying's Garden**
Monroe; 12 acres
flowers, vegetables

**Youngquist Farms**
Mount Vernon; 40 acres
berries

## FORAGER

**Foraged and Found Edibles**
Seattle
wild mushrooms, huckleberries,
wild greens

## FISH AND SEAFOOD

**Fishing Vessel *St. Jude***
Seattle
albacore tuna

**Taylor Shellfish Farms**
Shelton; 10,000 acres
clams, mussels, oysters, geoducks

**Two If By Seafoods**
Auburn
wild salmon

## PROCESSED FOODS

**Blue Cottage Jams**
Redmond
local fruit jam

**Booze Rubs**
Bellevue
all-natural seasoning blends

**La Pasta**
Seattle
artisan pasta and sauces

**Little Prague Bakery**
Seattle
European pastries

**Mt. Townsend Creamery**
Port Townsend
artisan cheese

**Pacific Coast Bakery**
Redmond
pastries and pies

**Pete's Perfect Toffee**
Mountlake Terrace
incredible toffee

**Preston Hill Bakery**
Preston
artisan breads

**Sound Bites**
Tacoma
hummus, pesto, chimichurri

**Sweet Sadie's Fudge Sauce**
Carnation
gourmet fudge sauce

**Tall Grass Bakery**
Seattle
artisan breads, cookies, granola

## PREPARED FOODS

**Anita's Crepes**
Seattle

**Hermosa Mexican Foods**
North Bend

**Poco Carretto Gelato**
Kirkland

**Veraci Pizza**
Seattle

# BIBLIOGRAPHY

Although I had stacks of books and articles at my side, the following were the most frequently used in helping me put together this creation.

Conran, Terence, and Caroline Conran. *The Cook Book*. London: Mitchell Beazley Publishers, 1980.

Fletcher, Janet. *Fresh from the Farmers' Market*. San Francisco: Chronicle Books, 1997.

Hirsheimer, Christopher, and Peggy Knickerbocker. *The San Francisco Ferry Plaza Farmers' Market Cookbook*. San Francisco: Chronicle Books, 2006.

Manning, Ivy. *The Farm to Table Cookbook: The Art of Eating Locally*. Seattle: Sasquatch Books, 2008.

Rombauer, Irma S., Marion Rombauer Becker, and Ethan Becker. *The Joy of Cooking*. New York: Scribner, 1997.

Saltsman, Amelia. *The Santa Monica Farmers' Market Cookbook*. Santa Monica: Blenheim Press, 2007.

Thomas, Cathy. *Melissa's Great Book of Produce*. Hoboken: John Wiley and Sons, Inc., 2006.

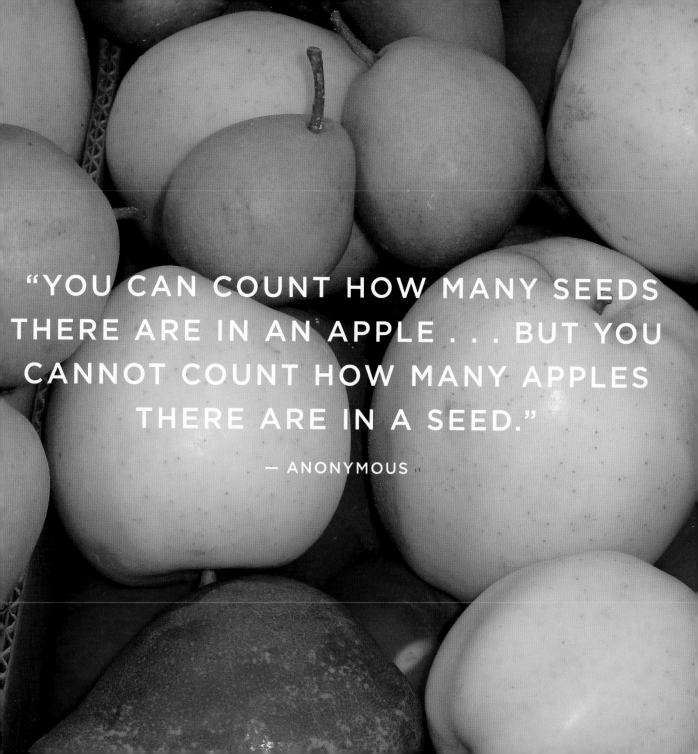

"YOU CAN COUNT HOW MANY SEEDS THERE ARE IN AN APPLE . . . BUT YOU CANNOT COUNT HOW MANY APPLES THERE ARE IN A SEED."

— ANONYMOUS

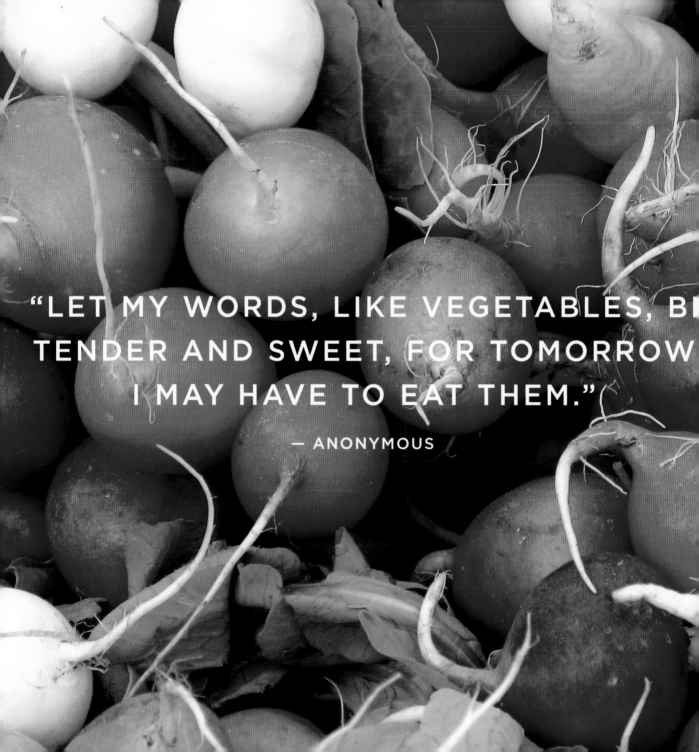

"LET MY WORDS, LIKE VEGETABLES, B[E] TENDER AND SWEET, FOR TOMORROW I MAY HAVE TO EAT THEM."

— ANONYMOUS

## ACKNOWLEDGMENTS

Let's start from the very beginning: a huge thanks to Lori Taylor for having the vision of a farmers' market in Bellevue. It has opened my eyes to a whole new world, and the community and I are healthier and wiser for her endeavor. I am grateful to the farmers who work alongside Mother Nature year-round and often travel great distances every week to share their farm-fresh bounty at the Market. Thanks to my sister-in-law Nora for going with me to the inaugural day of the Market and giving me my very own market bag for shopping. I was hooked! I want to thank my husband, Mark, for getting me in touch with book publisher Documentary Media, which changed me from saying, "I want to create a cookbook" to "I am creating a cookbook!" To Barry Provorse at Documentary Media, thanks for taking away my fear about, and sharing his enthusiasm for, a farmers' market cookbook. To publisher Petyr Beck, a huge thanks for guiding me through my maiden voyage in book publishing and making it such smooth sailing through uncharted waters. His calmness made it a very fun experience. My appreciation to Jon Cannell for his incredible talent at book design and his steady hand at carving the prints throughout this book. I was over the moon with delight seeing the words and images transformed into an art piece. Thanks to Judy Gouldthorpe for her editorial expertise in the culinary arts. I appreciate her keen attention to detail. I am grateful to all of my friends, especially Daniel, who became my guinea pigs in tasting my re-creations of the recipes. And, without the chefs and farmers who contributed their recipes, this cookbook would be only a dream. Thank you to all of them for taking time out of their busy schedules to share their cooking knowledge. A special thanks to Chef Holly Smith for writing the foreword, which made my day! Thanks to all of my family for their support and patience, especially Oliver, awaiting a walk in the park. I cannot forget to thank all of the geniuses at the Bellevue Square Apple Store for putting up with my almost weekly "not-so-genius" questions, teaching me about the many features of my Mac. And finally, thank YOU for supporting the Bellevue Farmers Market by shopping there and purchasing this book.

# INDEX

## A

albacore tuna, 98
apple tart, 94
apples, 74
applesauce, 94
apricot
    cheesecake, 40
    jam, 40
apricots, 16
apriums, 16
artichokes, 74
arugula, 16
arugula pesto, 116
Asian pears, 44
asparagus, 16
asparagus, grilled, with hazelnut aigrelette and Pinot
    Noir syrup, 30

## B

bamboo shoots, 18
basil pesto, 36, 112
Bavarian horseradish, 18
beans
    dried, in Italian bean soup, 104
    haricots verts, in Niçoise salad, 60
beans, dried, 98
beef
    pot roast, ginger, with vegetables and star anise, 92
    shepherd's pie, 114
    tenderloin with soy-Madeira glazed mushrooms, 34
beet soufflé, 31
beets, 18
berries
    pavlova with, 117
    strawberry-rhubarb crumble, 38
    in wild salmon salad with pomegranate vinaigrette, 66
blackberries, 44
blueberries, 44
bok choy, 18
bread salad (panzanella), 105
breads, storing, 98
broccoli, 18

broccoli rabe. *See* rapini
broccoli Romanesco, 44
broccoli Romanesco soup, 56

## C

cabbage, 74
cabbage
    kraut, fennel and, 91
    Savoy, and baby carrot salad, 108
    Savoy, in Italian bean soup, 104
carrot(s)
    baby, in ginger pot roast with vegetables and star
        anise, 92
    baby, salad, and Savoy cabbage, 108
    soup, 28
carrots, 19
cauliflower, 19
celeriac, parsnip, and turnip patties with tomatillo salsa,
    86
celery, 77
chard, 44
chard, rainbow, with edamame, 57
cheesecake, apricot, 40
cherries, 19
cherries
    Bing, with pan-seared salmon, 37
    pickled, mustard, 90
cider, 98
clams, steamed, with sweet basil pesto, 36
collards, 46
cookies, hazelnut shortbread, 118
corn, 77
corn
    cumin-spiked puree, with glazed pork tenderloin, 64
    salad, cherry tomato, 84
crumble, strawberry-rhubarb, 38
cucumber, in tabbouleh, 32
cucumbers, 19

## D

dandelion greens, 19
demi-glace, 91
desserts
    apple tart, 94
    apricot cheesecake, 40

hazelnut shortbread cookies, 118
pavlova with berries, 117
peach pie, 70
pear pocket pies, 67
poached tayberry pears, 68
pumpkin pie, 93
strawberry-rhubarb crumble, 38
dried beans, 98
dried fruit, 98

**E**

edamame, 46
edamame, with rainbow chard, 57
eggplant, 46
eggplant, in ratatouille, 62

**F**

fava beans, 20
fennel
    and cabbage kraut, 91
    with lobster mushrooms and tomato, 85
    in ratatouille, 62
    in roasted pepper soup, 102
fiddlehead ferns. *See* lady fern fiddleheads
figs, 77

**G**

garlic, 20
grapes, 77
greens with goat cheese and warm mushrooms, 106

**H**

haricots verts, 46
haricots verts, in Niçoise salad, 60
hazelnut
    aigrelette, 30
    shortbread cookies, 118
hazelnut oil, 99
hazelnuts, 99
herbs, fresh, 20
honey, 99
horseradish, 18
huckleberries, wild, 79

**J**

jam, apricot, 40
jams, 99

**K**

kale, 20
kale, in Italian bean soup, 104
kohlrabi, 21

**L**

lady fern fiddleheads, 21
lamb loins, cocoa nib crusted, 90
leeks, 21
lettuce, 21

**M**

marionberries, 46
meats, frozen, 98
melons, 47
mushrooms
    crimini, soy-Madeira glazed, 35
    dried, 98
    lobster, with fennel and tomato, 85
    morels, in English pea soup, 29
    shiitake, in ginger pot roast, 92
    wild, to clean, 51
    wild, in greens with goat cheese, 106
    wild, in risotto with spinach, 63
mussels Provençal, 89
mustard greens, 22

**N**

nectarines, 47

**O**

okra, 47
onion(s)
    pearl, in Savoy cabbage and baby carrot salad, 108
    soup, Dutch, 54
onions, 47

**P**

panzanella, 105

parsnip, turnip, and celeriac patties with tomatillo salsa, 86

parsnips, 78

pasta
    penne with fresh and roasted tomato sauce, 109
    ravioli, prepared, with arugula pesto, 116

pasta, frozen, 99

pavlova with berries, 117

pea soup, English, with minted ricotta and morels, 29

pea vines, 22

peach pie, 70

peaches, 48

pears, 48

pears, Asian, 44

pear(s)
    pies, pocket, 67
    poached tayberry, 68

peas, 22

penne with fresh and roasted tomato sauce, 109

peppers, 78

peppers, bell
    in ratatouille, 62
    roasted, 99
    roasted, soup, 102
    in tabbouleh, 32

pesto
    arugula, 116
    basil, 36
    Veraci, 112

pie
    crust, 71, 93
    peach, 70
    pear, 67
    pumpkin, 93

Pinot Noir syrup, with grilled asparagus, 30

pizza, thin-crust, 110

plums, 48

pluots, 48

pork tenderloin with cumin-spiked corn puree, 64

potatoes, 49

potatoes
    in ginger pot roast with vegetables and star anise, 92
    in Niçoise salad, 60

    in shepherd's pie, 114

pumpkin pie, 93

pumpkins, 79

purslane, 49

purslane salad, tomato and, 59

**R**

radicchio, 22

radishes, 22

rapini, 23

raspberries, 49

ratatouille, 62

ravioli, prepared, with arugula pesto, 116

rhubarb, 23

rhubarb crumble, strawberry, 38

rice, in risotto with spinach and wild mushrooms, 63

risotto with spinach and wild mushrooms, 63

**S**

salad
    bread, 105
    corn and cherry tomato, 84
    greens with goat cheese and warm mushrooms, 106
    Niçoise, 60
    panzanella, 105
    salmon with pomegranate vinaigrette, 66
    Savoy cabbage and baby carrot, 108
    tomato and purslane, 59

salad greens, 23, 49, 66

salad mix, 23

salmon
    frozen, 98
    pan-seared, and Bing cherries, 37
    salad with pomegranate vinaigrette, 66

salsa, tomatillo, 86

sea beans, 23

shepherd's pie, 114

sorrel, 23

soufflé, beet, 31

soup
    bean, Italian, 104
    broccoli Romanesco, 56
    carrot, 28
    Dutch onion, 54
    English pea, with minted ricotta and morels, 29
    roasted pepper, 102

tomato basil, 83
tomato, spicy, 83
winter squash, 82
spinach, 51
spinach, in risotto with wild mushrooms, 63
squash blossoms, 51
squash, summer, 24
squash, summer
blossom tempura, 58
zucchini, in ratatouille, 62
squash, winter, 79
squash, winter
pumpkin pie, 93
soup, 82
strawberries, 24
strawberry-rhubarb crumble, 38
sunchokes, 24

**T**
tabbouleh, 32
tart, apple, 94
tempura, summer squash blossom, 58
tomatillos, 78
tomatillos
in glazed pork tenderloin with cumin-spiked
corn puree, 64
salsa, 86
tomatoes, 78
tomatoes
cherry, with lobster mushrooms and fennel, 85
cherry, in salad, sweet corn, 84
in mussels Provençal, 89
penne with fresh and roasted tomato sauce, 109
in ratatouille, 62
roasted, 109
in salad, bread, 105
salad, corn and, 84
in salad, Niçoise, 60
in salad, with purslane, frisée, 59
sauce, fresh, 109
soup, basil, 83
soup, spicy, 83
in tabbouleh, 32

tuna, albacore, 98
tuna, smoked, in Niçoise salad, 60
turnip, parsnip, and celeriac patties with tomatillo salsa,
86
turnips, 79

**V**
vinaigrette, pomegranate, 66
vinegar, storing, 99

**W**
watercress, 24
wild mushrooms, 51
wine, 99

**Y**
yu choy, 79

**Z**
zucchini, in ratatouille, 62

# TABLE OF EQUIVALENTS

## LIQUID / DRY MEASUREMENTS

1 pinch = 1/8 teaspoon

3 teaspoons = 1 tablespoon = 1/2 ounce

2 tablespoons = 1/8 cup = 1 ounce

4 tablespoons = 1/4 cup = 2 ounces

16 tablespoons = 1 cup = 8 ounces = 1/2 pound

2 cups = 1 pint = 16 ounces = 1 pound

2 pints = 1 quart = 32 ounces = 2 pounds

4 quarts = 1 gallon = 128 ounces = 8 pounds

1 peck of pickled peppers = 10-14 pounds

4 pecks = 1 bushel and a hug around the neck

## FOOD EQUIVALENTS (APPROXIMATE)

**Apple**
1 medium = 1 cup sliced

**Apricot**
1 pound = 8-10 whole

**Broccoli**
1 pound = 4 cups florets

**Butter**
1 stick = 1/2 cup = 1/4 pound

**Cabbage**
1 pound = 4 cups shredded

**Carrot**
1 medium = 1/2 cup chopped

**Celery**
1 stalk = 1/2 cup chopped

**Clams**
6-12 per serving, depending on size

**Corn**
2 medium ears = 1 cup kernels

**Cucumber**
1 medium = 1 cup chopped

**Dried beans**
1 pound dried = 2 cups dried = 6 cups cooked

**Fish (fillet/steak)**
6-8 ounces per serving, uncooked

**Garlic**
1 small clove = 1/2 teaspoon minced

**Green onion**
1 medium = 2 tablespoons sliced

**Herbs**
1 cup fresh = 1/3 cup dried = 1/4 cup ground

**Kale**
1 pound raw = 2 cups cooked

**Leek**
1 medium = 1/3 cup sliced

**Lemon**
1 medium = 2-3 tablespoons juice

**Meat**
1/2 pound per serving, uncooked

**Mussels**
12-15 per serving

**Onion**
1 medium = 1/2 cup chopped

**Oysters**
6-12 per serving, depending on size

**Parsnip**
1 medium = 1 cup chopped

**Pasta**
1 pound uncooked = 1 1/4 pounds cooked = 4-5 servings

**Peach**
2 medium = 1 cup sliced

**Peas in pod**
1 pound in pod = 1 cup shelled

**Potato**
1 pound = 3 medium = 3 cups sliced = 2 cups mashed

**Rhubarb**
1 pound = 4 cups sliced

**Soup**
1 cup per serving = appetizer;
1 1/2-2 cups per serving = main course

**Spinach**
1 1/2 pounds fresh = 1 cup cooked;
1 1/2 pounds raw for salad = 4 servings

**Strawberries**
1 pint = 1 pound = 3 cups whole = 2 1/2 cups sliced

**Sweet pepper**
1 medium = 3/4 cup chopped

**Tomato**
1 medium = 1 cup chopped

**Winter squash**
2 pounds = 4 cups chopped = 2 cups pureed

**Zucchini**
1 medium = 1 1/2 cups sliced

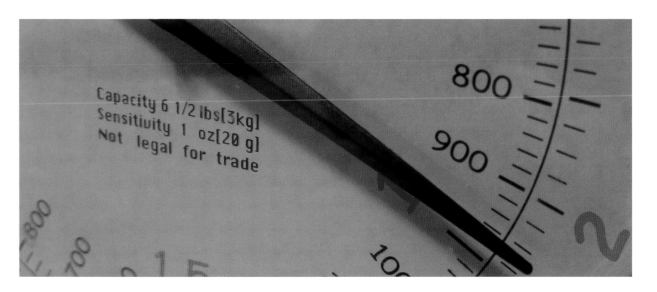